Deviled Egg Report

Deviled Egg Report

CHAN

ISBN 978-1-452-81085-0

FIRST EDITION

This book is dedicated to my eternal friends, Dan and Jerry, who inspired me and helped me in my hard times . . . .

CONTENTS

PART 5. BRAIN WORK

PART 6. REBUILDING TIME

PART 7. GOING GLOBAL

INTRODUCTION

When I was young, in elementary school, my Dad thought I would become a Dean of College or a Judge for having sparkling eyes and being keen. My aptitude test indicated that I should become a surgeon (followed by a librarian). We were pretty poor after my Dad passed away, and there was no way for my Mom to support me through the medical school (nor had I a burning desire to become a surgeon).

I decided to become an engineer, for the challenge, but my teacher didn't approve of my application for the college entrance exam as an Electronics Engineering major. "What!? Electronics Engineering!? Engineering is not a good field for a girl," he snorted, "You will not be able to get a job." I entered Yon-Sei University, one of the best private universities in Korea, as the Chemistry major.

The idea of becoming a teacher as my Mom advised or a scientist working at some pharmaceutical or cosmetic company lab didn't appeal to me. That didn't seem challenging enough, but I enjoyed hanging around with boy classmates, drinking beers and joking around, enjoying the new freedom out of strict all girl high school disciplines and the attention of new gender friends, playing the coolest girl who knew the best disco clubs in town.

I didn't have much interest in what was expected of me, a housewife or limited opportunities for women in Korea, and I decided to adventure to America and discover my future. I switched major to Electrical and Computer Engineering with emphasis on Communications, and I was lucky enough to get my co-op position with Unisys (it was Burroughs then, before having merged with Sperry), despite my below-average verbal communication skill (I did have high GPA).

My verbal communication skill was still relatively poor when I was graduating from Drexel University, and nobody seemed interested in hiring me as an engineer. I continued to pursue my future career as an engineer, and as I was completing my graduate coursework, I got an intern-job offer with an organization supporting military IT operations in Washington DC. Many had thought it would be hard for me to get started as an engineer, being an Asian female and even new to the States, and I was thankful to be able to land an engineering job.

I was fairly naïve during my DSIA years, much more so than my peers grew up in America. My superiors and colleagues treated me well though for being polite, well-educated and eager to contribute. They were very generous and forgiving of my mistakes. I just worked conscientiously and kept my mind open for new professional world. And after 2-3 years, I had become a rising star of the organization with the top management supporting me eagerly.

A star was born there, as a matter of fact, having been assigned as the key member of the most visible and complex project and completing it successfully, but I wanted to explore other opportunities. After working for DSIA for six years, I adventured out to private industry, and from one job after another, I learned that my male colleagues were appreciating me more for my look than my engineering skills, sometimes even covering my lack of engineering skills, happily. They were just happy to have me around, even better if I needed their help to do my job . . .

Before I realized how far I had come to in my engineering career, an interviewer at Booz Allen, one of the most prestigious IT consulting firms, said to me, "I have never seen anybody with a background like this," surprising me. "Fantastic!" he kept saying. So, there I was, the best candidate for the US Department of Defense networking, with nobody even close to me (except those who didn't need to look for a new job).

My philosophy, whether it is personal or professional, has always been "know yourself" as Socrates said some thousand years ago, and "the best thing you can do is to be yourself" as my first boss advised me with the best intention. And it had worked for me, for every challenging or difficult situation.

With trouble rejoining DSIA as the Devil, my story has been vaguely broadcasted by many television shows and radio channels, and everyone seemed to be going wild with the idea of back. It surprised me that people were so fascinated by my story. I was interested in using the air media to see how general people would react to my situation. Then I became the prisoner of the media with people's demand to know what's going on with me . . . . *"You can check in any time you like~, but you can never l~e~a~ve~~~"*

What I could see being reflected on television is that too many people are operating based on the *ego*, with no analysis of themselves (how they are perceived by others). Years ago, a friend of mine told me that I was living in my own world. I was wrapped around my own ego, only seeing what I wanted to see. I wasn't seeing myself with someone else's eyes, placing myself in the big picture or the overall social structure. My friend was being diplomatic and considerate of my feelings not to say that I was being a knucklehead, operating with "me-view," only, the view that made me feel good. What he told me didn't even register into my thick head then.

Perhaps people are aware of their shortcomings, but they don't want to admit their shortcomings in order to satisfy their ego. No improvement can be made in that case, just like an alcoholic needing to see himself (or herself) having a drinking problem. I was fortunate enough to meet many who helped me open my eyes to see myself.

I am thankful to America for giving me many chances, possibly more than I deserved in some ways. Many have been very generous, allowing me to come a long way. I am sure that some people never had been given same chances that I had been given . . . .

I have written my story to share my experience, and hopefully, everyone will learn something through my wide-open 4 eyes or get some good laughs. Someone said to me when I was walking down the street of Philadelphia, "We could all use your laugh!"

This book is composed of snapshots of my professional experience as a female IT engineer and my email collections describing how I have become known as the Devil . . . . It is divided into seven parts in chronological order, consisting of independent episodes from my first job to my last job. The first five parts are my professional experience, focused on people who I met and various situations I had dealt with on the job. The 6th part is how my situation has led to initiate the back position and what happened trying to join an organization supporting military IT operations (described as emails to my sister and some friends), how I got connected then trapped to the air against my will (described as emails). The 7th part is for moving into the global community joining a foreign-based company and some thoughts on harmony and happiness . . . . ?

This is a straight story just as I experienced and saw . . . .

*Company names are *Da Vinci* coded and the individual's names changed to protect their privacy.

Making of FIRE

PART 1

WORK SHOULD BE FUN

MY FIRST PROJECT

My first project was to develop a prototype expert system that would diagnose military data communications problems. It was a new concept that my boss was trying to determine if it was viable to apply the new artificial intelligence technology to troubleshoot the malfunctioning of the military IT baseline systems.

The project leader, Chuck, was like a typical government employee, a relaxed and easy-going guy. He always came to work carrying a huge bagful of things, although it didn't look like he was using what he carried around to work, whatever they were. I shared an office with him, and we went to lunch together sometimes. He lived about 5 minutes away from where I lived, driving distance, almost like a neighbor. Chuck was full of something but definitely not one of the sharpest guys around.

Nobody in this group knew anything about the expert system or artificial intelligence, and I was expected to be the technical lead introducing this new technology to the group, for having taken one class when I was in graduate school.

My boss, Pete, was a 40-year old bachelor, who majored the Mathematics, and he was known as one of the best operating systems analysts for the military command and control systems. Pete was a clean and sharp-looking guy but not exactly attractive looking with the front half of his hairs gone and everything. He looked like a picky and nagging type, munching celeries and carrots for lunch, like one of those guys trying hard to keep their heart or lung pink or something, a health-nut kind. He made me think of Galileo, for some reason, probably because of his Italian heritage, his look or mathematician-like behaviors. He was sincere and professional, except he often tried to laugh too hard for things that he obviously didn't think was all that funny, trying too hard to make himself appeal as he had a terrific sense of humor, making himself looking rather goofy.

Pete was not the manager who hired me. I was hired through the intern program along with 10-15 other new graduates, and we had been given a tour to a number of DSIA facilities and placed based on the needs and/or the individual's preference. I had requested that I would prefer to work at the Center For Engineering (CFE) and got placed in his group, at the Operational Support Facility (OSF), an off-site of the CFE.

I worked closely with a Honeywell communications systems expert, Steve Jones, who was very friendly, tall, 6'2" or so, and had genuine nice guy smile that showed he had a warm heart. He was the best (the highest ranking) in his field of military communications systems, and I interviewed him to collect his problem-solving techniques. What was really noticeable of him was his bright blonde hair that almost looked too rich, kind of like 24K gold color. I thought, 'Geez, American guys have some bright goldy hair, too.' Then I noticed one day that his growing hair was dark brown. I didn't know men dyed their hairs until then.

Steve was popular with women, especially with middle-aged shameless spunky government-employee women who wouldn't hesitate to attack a man, although he seemed to prefer to play around with younger and pretty females or a naïve foreigner like me . . . Some people referred him as "Mr. Casanova," for good reason(s).

He was more than helpful and buoyant, sometimes trying a little too hard, moving his fingers on my flow chart to show "yes" goes this way, "no" goes that way. It was my chart and I knew exactly which way was yes- and which way was no-direction. "I think I can figure out the yes-or-no direction myself," I told him, looking into his eyes questioning his reason for doing that. "Oh, I didn't mean to do that," he said, smiling.

"When a customer contacts you reporting that their system's response is slow, how would you resolve the situation?" He answered, "I would ask if they have a monitoring system, and if yes," dragging his finger to the yes-direction on my chart again, and I couldn't help laughing at his over-helping. "Ha ha ha," he laughed, too, realizing his own behavior by my laugh, "Oh, I did it again!"

Steve was a totally fun-loving kind of guy, who had hopped around the male bars in Seoul, Bangkok, and singing at karaoke in Okinawa. Some men were jealous of him working with me, the brand new intern, flirting and visiting me in my cubicle to joke around (while they couldn't).

On a Friday afternoon, he came by and sat in my cubicle making himself comfortable to chat for a while . . . And it led to a story of him eating a fresh-catched small fish, alive, how he could feel the fish wriggling in his stomach, wriggling his fingers on his stomach so that I would get a clear picture of what was going on in his stomach. I screamed, looking at his fingers, "**Eu aah aak~ ahh!!!!!~~~**", startling him. I was so absorbed into his gross wriggling that I forgot where I was. People came over to see what in the world was happening . . . One of his friends, a sarcastic guy with sharp tongue, scoffed, "You guys are having too much fun!"

I didn't like this guy very much. Dick was his name. He was too cynical, I always thought, negative and defiant about everything, acting like he was too smart for the place with less competent people. He probably thought I was a dunno-better naïve young chick, getting hooked by his bad Casanova friend's charm. A cute but stupid foreigner. He referred me as a snow bunny when he saw me driving back to work at the lunch time on a heavy snowy day. He often came to my cubicle when Steve was there, joking about the middle-aged women employees for the group as "honey, I am bored" kind and telling me how he was more focused on his other home-based business/project work.

Steve was a good friend with my Galileo boss, who didn't seem too thrilled about Steve visiting my cubicle and joking around with me. Pete came by my cubicle one day to ask me how my project was going, then out of blue, he said, "People are not out to get you." I didn't have a clue why he said that to me, I never thought anyone was out to get me? Maybe I appeared too uptight to some people, to him? I was new, and I wasn't going around visiting other cubicles to make friends, just saying "hi" to others who I happened to run into here and there. I didn't say anything, puzzled, trying to figure why he was saying that to me, and he said, "The best thing you can do is to be yourself."

Steve caught me reading an expert system manual, with my face on the desk, like I was about to fall asleep. "Lazy, lazy, you are reading the manual now to develop the system? I see where this is going. Ha Ha~" I had to read the manual to figure out how to use the expert system tool that we had selected, and reading a thick manual was making me sleepy. Others would have fallen asleep, I was one of the more awaken ones there, actually.

Sometimes I visited Steve's cubicle mostly to clarify the interviews I had with him. I walked over to Steve's cubicle to talk about the schedule, and he was looking at his calendar. My eyes followed his eyes naturally, and to my embarrassment, he had one of those naked women calendar! Totally naked, that was! I did not want to be looking at this naked woman picture with him. I certainly didn't expect to see anything like that hanging at the office! I could feel my face was getting hot. "I'll be back later," I mumbled and turned away quickly. He looked puzzled, then I heard him laughing hard behind my back, HA HA HA~~~

One day, Mr. Erdman, the Director, came by my cubicle and asked me how I was doing with my expert system work. I was delighted for his visit first, then his knowledge and experience in the expert system. I thought nobody in this building knew what this new technology was about, and there he was, understanding exactly what I was doing. He said, "**Work should be fun**." I was surprised (and delighted) that this as-dry-as-one-gets top executive made such a remark to me, an intern, the bottom-of-the-bread-chain nobody. (I ran into him at a Kmart one day, but he didn't seem too thrilled by that though).

The prototype expert system was developed, and a demonstration of the system to the Front Office Executives, Mr. Erdman and his right- and left-hand men, Mr. Myers and Mike Pucillo, respectively, was setup. It was the first time I saw Mr. Myers, and he was sitting all the way back rather than taking a seat right behind the demo system like the other two executives.

My teammate, a Vietnamese-French female who brought in to work with me on this project as a GS-12 Computer Scientist, got very nervous, trembling and stuttering, despite her several years of industry experience. Everyone in the room looked concerned, and I could just imagine what they were all thinking, "the nervous, tiny Asian female!"

I was a little nervous watching Huyen not performing well, but once I took the demo seat, I was like a pro! Before I started, I asked Mr. Myers if he could see the demo screen well enough from the back, and he said he was just fine. I went through the prepared procedures calmly. "Let's say the fault type is XP," but my finger hit the option below, OM, "or OM," I quickly changed, continuing with my demo like I intended to hit OM. I knew, of course, that either XP or OM would take me to the same steps, the steps that I almost memorized. Still, I was cooler than I knew. "Whatever your finger says, huh?" Chuck commented.

After the demo, Pete told me that I was super, and Chuck gave me a nervous look with a little twisted mouth, re-evaluating me, looking at me up and down. I was only a GS-9 Computer Engineer going through the Intern program. I felt terrific!

We had a few more demonstrations to various groups to determine whether to develop a full-blown system or not. The prototype expert system incorporating several experts' problem-solving techniques actually performed better than any one of the experts, and the experts, including Steve, became reluctant to provide their expertise after they had seen the demo. So my first task ended, just having developed the prototype.

Through this task, I gained very favorable professional reputation as a cool, smart and renovating engineer capable of carrying on a difficult task without guidance. Everyone in the group treated me as a top-notch engineer who would contribute to the group with new and advanced technologies.

One day, I ran into Mr. Erman and his right-hand man, Mr. Myers. I was wearing a soft cotton white shirt with asymmetrical wavy collar and navy pants, my self-satisfied work dress-up style for these days. Both of them stared at me momentarily, almost stopped walking and stopped breathing, like they had seen something amazing. It was a typical simple male professional look with a bit of feminine touch.

From their reaction, I sensed that one's look might have a bigger impact on men in the working world, even in the dry engineering field. They not only would appreciate someone pleasing to their eyes (wishing attractive females to do well) regardless of their level, but also they would prefer "professionally" attractive females, possibly giving more chances . . . . ?

MR. BIG HEART

Mike Pucillo, one of my strongest supporters at the OSF, brought me a crème my sister had custom-made for my face, for fading brown spots. He had gone through a lot of trouble, keeping the crème in the refrigerator in Japan and Hawaii. Then he got caught at the airport by a dog sniffing at his luggage bag with my crème in, and his name got entered into the computer.

"What the hell was that for?" He inquired me when he returned to the office, "It'd better be something worth all this trouble I had gone through." I was a little embarrassed to tell him that it was for my stupid little face thing and just laughed. "It was for removing the brown spots," I had to tell him when he asked again seriously, pointing the brown spots on my face. "Ha ha~ you don't need to try to remove those spots, you look cute enough."

Later, his assistant Brigid, a GS-14 woman manager, came by and asked me what the crème that Mike brought me from Korea was for . . . "Oh, for that!" She laughed and told me that she had some great crème for removing the brown spot her husband had brought from Saudi Arabia, and she would bring it to me the following day. Apparently, Mike had been going around the building telling people about the trouble he had trying to bring me some crème from Korea.

That afternoon, Mr. Harry Myers walked out of the office, and he didn't return to the office the next day or the following day or the day after . . . Margarette, Communications and Networking Group Manager who was playing the Diva of this group, gave me a look, which I read as 'This is new, what the hell is this girl doing to men?'

Mike had always been very friendly and supportive of me, but when I asked him to help me get the system I needed for some testing, he snapped, "You got someone better than me who will take care of you." What I could figure was that Mr. Myers and Mike were doing some kind of male-ego competition over me. I called Mr. Myers at home, and he answered the call, "hello?" "......" "hello?" "......" I didn't really have anything urgent that required his attention immediately and hung up. I just felt I needed to call him.

On my birthday, I thought I should have lunch with someone special and called Harry Myers, who became my favorite guy there, after calling him at home and everything. I thought he would be thrilled by my birthday lunch invitation, but he sounded very cold, "What can I help you with?" Ouch. All of sudden, I felt tiny. My confidence disappeared quickly and I just wanted to hang up the stupid phone, but I already said that it was me when he answered the call. "A-h-, it's nothing important. Today is my birthday and i was wondering if you would like to have lunch with me . . . " I couldn't even hear him breathing for a few seconds, then he said slowly, "oh,,, " His voice sounded warmer but I could feel he was feeling awkward by my birthday call and quickly said, "I am sorry, I didn't mean to bother you. Bye."

It felt like I'd just made a fool out of myself. I felt like an idiot!!! My face felt hot with my dumb call. Maybe he wasn't really interested in me, he just wanted to prove that he was the BOSS!

A few days later, I saw Mr. Myers driving behind me, on my way back home. My heart jumped, and I kept looking at the back-mirror trying to determine whether he was following me or he was just going somewhere that happened to be in the same direction, kept wondering whether I should pull the car over or continue driving . . . Then I thought about making a turn and see if he made the same turn, too, which would mean he was following me . . .

'I'd better stop looking at the back mirror so often, he can probably see me looking at the back-mirror,' I told myself and kept driving . . . I could feel my heart beat, 'kung-quang kung-quang, kung-quang kung-quang,' I tried to restrain myself from looking at the back-mirror and kept driving, and after passing several blocks, I looked at the back-mirror, and he was gone (Whew~).

Margarette assigned me as an installation team member to go to Korea, to install the system that I modified as the Tiger Team task. Two most notorious playboys at the OSF building, Steve and Bill, were on my team, and people were joking that my team would have an orgy in Korea.

I knew Steve, the Honeywell communications expert who helped me develop an expert system, but I didn't have chance to work with Bill, who was with DSIA, a different group at the other side of the building. Steve and Bill were buddies, both in their 40's with similar playboyish mood and fun-loving personalities, and they seemed pretty excited about the trip. The team was making the travel reservation together, but since both Steve and Bill had been to Korea many times for other installation trips, I decided to travel alone and meet them in Korea.

I saw Mr. Myers standing around at my side of building, which he seldom came in, and he looked at me with worried expression on his face. I just passed by him, wondering what was on his mind . . . ? That afternoon, the installation trip to Korea got cancelled. It would have been my first business trip to Korea and I was looking forward to this trip. I was a little disappointed, but at the same time, I felt relieved. No more orgy-gossip or my playboy teammates' meaningful smiles at each other . . .

I was playing Mahjongg when one of my teammates, an Air Force Major, Chris, swung by my cubicle, asking me if I was going to attend the all-hands meeting. Chris was a reserved but witty single guy in his 40's. It was a meeting hosted by Mr. Harry Myers to inform everyone of a new Technology Insertion Project (TIP), testing and integrating new client-server architecture-based application developed by the DARPA.

Lisa, a blonde from California who was managing the LAN test-bed with Van Dyke contractors, had been selected as a DSIA engineer to setup a test-bed and to coordinate this initiative with the DARPA members. She was sitting at the front row of the large theater-like conference room gloriously. I noticed Harry had changed his hair style to all-back, looking like a sleek swindler. He used to look like a classy guy, rather handsome and solid looking, I thought, but with his new hair-do, he looked like a bad guy and looked unnatural, almost goofy.

As I was wondering about his new hair-do (guessing that he was trying to hook-up with Lisa), Chris whispered to me, "Why did he comb his hair that way?" I burst into laugh and had to hide behind the chair so that Mr. Myers wouldn't see me laughing at him. Chris was laughing, too, looking at me laughing like crazy, even choking trying not to make any noise.

Lisa came to the lab and said, "You use everything you've got to get what you want, right? I knew exactly what she was up to. I didn't say anything, just gave her a look, 'Bitch!' Lisa was very intelligent and had a Venus statue-like pretty face, tall with slim body. She was good looking, but her whining voice wasn't exactly attractive, rather annoying. She was trying very hard to beat me, always trying to prove that she knew more than me, saying "My rival at my previous job was a graduate of Cornell University." I thought she was trying too hard to impress others how much she knew, trying to cover her lack of education.

A few days later, Lisa came in looking gorgeous, with her hair-up and wearing a very spiffy suite with a short skirt, showing her nice long legs. I was standing in front of the building chatting with a bunch of people during the lunch time and saw Mr. Hotshot in his car waiting for someone, then Lisa came out, got into his car, and they drove off . . .

I had seen him going to lunch with Margarctte sometimes, but the atmosphere was different. It looked more like a date than a casual working lunch. I bumped into him later that day, and he said, "I am sorry." It was more than 'sorry, bumping,' I sensed. It sounded more like 'sorry, dumping' before I had chance to do anything with him, after having generated all the rumors. JERK!

Soon after, Mr. Myers and Lisa went to Germany for some meeting. Lisa must have coordinated the meeting to take a trip with him, no doubt. She was more than capable of doing things like that. I felt a little sad when Harry said sorry, almost felt like crying, but I got over quickly. I just continued to do my task like nothing happened. Nothing happened as a matter of fact. It was just people's perception (of him might be attracted to me) and some gossips.

Lisa came to see me when she returned from her trip and said, "Only stupid gives all the way!" I didn't ask her what happened, I didn't want to know. I figured that Mr. Big Heart didn't care for her calculated seduction. Then she said, "I need more sex appeal," studying my look. 'Whatever', I thought. I wasn't trying to be sexy, and it probably had little to do with her sex appeal. She was trying too hard to impress him, probably.

Next day, the TIP Project Manager and Chris came by to tell me that we had a meeting with Mr. Myers in his office. Mr. Cool-pants was in a very good mood, super friendly, going through some briefing charts, describing each and every single pages in details. He kept looking at me like he was wondering how I was feeling, I could sense. I was thrilled by that, but I didn't take my eyes off of the briefing charts on the table, trying not to make an eye contact with him, 'not as you wish, Mr. Casanova Polite?!,'

Lisa came into the meeting room next morning looking like she had been crying all night long. Chris must have told her about my meeting with Mr. Myers, and she must have figured that she got dumped and felt sorry for herself. Too bad. Obviously, she was interested in becoming Harry's favorite, hoping that it would accelerate her to move up the ladder, even pushing it. After the meeting, she came by my cubicle and said to me, "I don't play with love." ('Huh? Does that mean I play with love?')

I didn't tell her that she's gotta win man's heart one way or another. Pushing man with sex didn't get her what she wanted, obviously, not with Mr. Big Heart! Apparently, big guys with good heart like Harry Myers are compassionate for someone vulnerable who they can provide protection, not interested in those who tried to use them for moving up.

After his short trip to Germany with Lisa, Mr. Myers and Lisa seemed to try to avoid each other if at all possible. Lisa continued her test-bed management work, taking trips with military officers at the Pentagon, bragging (or bitching) me about them.

Mr. Myers, who owned the building by this time, respected and popular with his good leadership, became a very strong supporter of me for my new task, Technology Insertion Project that changed my professional status from a technology-savvy intern to the "Dragon Lady" . . .

TECHNOLOGY INSERTION PROJECT

After Lisa had tested a DARPA-developed client-server application on her test-bed successfully, I was assigned to serve as the Infrastructure Engineer for Technology Insertion Project (TIP). It was to transition Honeywell mainframe-oriented operating environment into the TCP/IP network centered client-server architecture. A client-server application developed by the DARPA and three applications used by the Army, Navy and Air Force, independently, were to be integrated as the first set of the client-server joint applications, and 31 military command and control systems sites spread worldwide were selected as the initial operating sites, with three beta sites for the Army, Navy and Air Force operations.

Mr. Arambulo, the Project Manager, took me to the ASR, the TIP prime contractor, to introduce me to the contractor team members. They presented me with a draft site survey template, and even with a quick review, I could tell that it was lacking several key information needed to engineer the network for the TIP fielding. I made a few sharp comments on their sloppy work. Nobody was able to answer my inquiry or had anything to say about my comments. A female engineer, a formal onsite contractor to DSIA, who apparently joined the ASR for this new task, mumbled an excuse, "That's why it's a draft . . ."

The ASR Task Manager quickly went out and brought in a guy and introduced him to me as the networking expert. I had seen him at the OSF building before but I didn't know what he was doing there, just assumed him as one of many on-site contractors. Apparently he had left his old post and joined the TIP team as a subcontractor supporting the ASR. His name was Dan Cornwell, and he clarified the issues I brought up without hesitation. 'At least someone knew what they were doing,' I thought.

After the meeting, I spent some time in Dan's office, discussing the military network architecture. I learned that he had worked at the OSF as an on-site sales engineer for Honeywell, and he knew that I had developed an expert system, had seen me playing mahjongg on my PC several times walking by my cubicle. So he already knew me more than enough.

I distributed the draft survey template to DSIA networking experts for comments, and Lisa was pretty disgusted, calling it a "piece of crap!" Just by Lisa's comments alone, the survey template needed a serious rework, just as I had thought. I formed a survey template development team consisting of DSIA networking experts and ASR members including Lisa and Dan as key engineers.

At my first meeting, a tall guy showed up, introducing himself as the TIP Integration Manager, John Scott. He looked like a gentleman, a smart gentleman wearing glasses, and he was very knowledgeable in the military operating environment. He spoke very softly, and I liked him immediately, his manners and knowledge, easy-going personality, smoothness . . . He looked like a totally nice and generous guy, bigger than everyone with overall warm mood, and I was pretty pleased with him being my partner-in-crime besides his young manager, Mark.

I met frequently with John, Mark, and Dan for the survey template at the ARS facility in addition to the regular meeting with every team members at the DSIA building. During one of my visits to the ARS facility, I ran into John, and we chatted for a while. He was very witty and sarcastic about the government, making me burst into laugh. I turned around to laugh, so I wouldn't look goofy (looking too happy, like a bimbo), and he laughed, "Huh huh huh" like a big guy with lots of space. There, we clicked instantly!

Later, John offered me to join his group as a systems administrator, but I was doing pretty well with DSIA and I didn't want to take a chance. He was in a position to please me as a contractor, but as a boss, he could be different or even abusive. I did hear some bad comments about him as a manager who managed people by fear, from some guys working for him.

An 80-page site survey template was developed, and the first three teams were scheduled to survey three beta sites. I assigned myself for the Army site in Georgia to conduct survey with a DSIA senior member, Bob, and two ARS people, Mark and his assistant. It was my first survey, and I felt uneasy with big responsibility on my shoulder as the lead for the overall survey.

My survey team got together for dinner, and as we were checking menus, John showed up at the restaurant. I was happy to see him, feeling relieved. I didn't have much confidence in Mark covering me well enough when I faltered. John was much more experienced in this environment, having served in the Air Force for 20-some years. He had just surveyed a Navy site in Virginia with Lisa, so he was the best hand for this.

The conference room was full with 20-25 site representatives attending our in-brief. Bob briefed everyone on the purpose of our visit, and John answered most of the questions, as I had hoped. After the meeting, I asked John, "What do you think?" and he said, "It's going to be a little more challenging than the ACOM." He had to cover the questions Lisa answered at the ACOM, that meant, I figured. But he already knew that, and that was probably why he came, unscheduled, to cover me and his young manager, the new clueless ones in the military environment leading the survey task.

Luckily, this site had a very knowledgeable and experienced network administrator, who had a soft heart on me, as he said. I understood the technology well enough, and it was just a matter of obtaining the site infrastructure information (filling out the survey templates that "I" developed). Still, a knowledgeable network administrator would make it much easier to fill out the form, and this administrator provided not only the information that I had asked for (without any difficulty), but also volunteered some other information with some suggestions for modifying our survey template. This site had an unusual infrastructure, and that needed to be incorporated as well.

John hung around with me while I was collecting the infrastructure information, carrying on conversations with customers. Mark and his contractor collected the operational information, and Bob walked around the building chatting with different customers.

In the evening, the team hopped around the restaurants and bars. After dinner, Mark split from the group with his contractor babe.. I hung around with Bob and John, and Bob wasn't interested in staying out late. Bob was an old man in his 60s who needed to go to bed early.

John and I walked around Atlanta for two nights, stopping at a bar for a few more drinks. When we went to the same bar the second time, the bartender remembered what I drank the first time I was there, "whisky sour?" John laughed and asked him, "Do you remember what I drank?" The bartender bluntly said, "No." After a few drinks, I felt like teasing John, so I sat on his lap. He was thrilled, I must say, smiling ear-to-ear, "I am going to Korea with you."

Upon return, I wrote a special survey report presenting the problem with this site's infrastructure with a recommendation of changes needed to operate properly in the TIP environment. In addition, I recommended DSIA to establish a central authority to assign and manage legal IP addresses for the TIP sites having discovered that this site was using illegal IP addresses.

My Division Manager was more than pleased with my report. Lisa had been visiting this site every few months to work on the networking issues, but she didn't see the problem, merely exchanging networking device information, testing the devices that this site used for the TIP. He almost ran to the Front Office with my report, giving me a thumb up. I was selected for this task for having the right education (vs. someone with more experience in the military environment), and I was on my way to become a star player for transforming the DoD infrastructure used for over 30 years.

SURVEY TRIPS TO MILITARY INSTALLATIONS

With the experience surveying three beta sites, I planned to form three teams to conduct the site surveys for 31 military sites, and everyone was excited about the survey trips, wishing to be selected for the sites referred as golden sites such as Hawaii or Europe. I thought I should accompany Mr. Myers for a survey or two since I was responsible for the overall survey, keeping everyone on the team reasonably happy, including him who was the Head of this project. I was under the pressure I put on myself, more or less.

Harry Myers often visited sites in Europe and would be a good leader for the European theater, but I didn't think Europe would be a good choice for me to survey. I would be better received by the Pacific theater and Korea, I assumed. Mr. Myers agreed to visit some sites in Europe, but he declined to visit Korea, recommending some other senior member.

During an in-process review briefing to customers, ARS contractors were gossiping about Mr. Arambulo, the Project Manager transferring to Pentagon. "We have a new boss," the ARS Task Manager said, looking at me and speculating that it might have something to do with the conflict between me and Mr. Arambulo. It was rather happy news to me as I didn't care for him. He looked like one of those academic nerds, talking with goofy rumbling voice, and he seemed to prefer to have either Lisa or Chris instead of me.

One of the DSIA team member, an older lady, was angry and almost screamed at me, "It's your fault," when nobody had the answer for one of the issues that we were discussing at a meeting with ARS. I just gave her, 'Don't be ridiculous' look. She was the one who the old Project Manager brought into the team. Apparently, some people must have thought it was me who chased him out of this project. I had never said anything negative about Mr. Arambulo to anyone. He was more negative about me.

The new Project Manager, Lieutenant Colonel Segrest came on board shortly. He was with Army, who looked like a nice teacher, wearing glasses, with warm smile. LTC Segrest was an excellent speaker, eloquent, confident and firm. He reminded me of my Dad in many ways, in overall mood, and I welcomed this change. He seemed like a straightforward, a very mature man with good military discipline, who would treat me fairly. No nonsense kind of man.

Mr. Myers and Chris, an Air Force Major, were to lead the survey team for sites in Germany and England. I assumed the team would visit sites together, but Mr. Myers went to those sites by himself, briefed the customers before his team arrived and returned to the office within a few days. Apparently, he just hopped around sites as quickly as he could, just doing what he needed to do without his team. He was probably too high for his team members, playing 'lonely at the top' thing, possibly.

I surveyed a few sites in Washington DC area first, alone for small sites and accompanied by Bob and/or ARS engineers for larger sites, practicing my survey skills and getting familiar with military operations. After one of the surveys, the snow was falling down hard as Bob and I were on our way back home. It was getting dark and I couldn't see a darn thing in front of me, yet Bob wasn't turning his windshield-wipers on. I swung my hand left and right, trying to remind him of the snow wiping car tool, looking at him. He opened a window, stretched his hand out and swung the windshield wiper with his hand, left and right, as he was driving. Holy cow! Geez! Ha Ha Ha~. It was so him, totally relaxed and goofy. I laughed hard, and he said, "My wife drives a nice car."

Bob and two ARS people, John and his go-for Tom, accompanied me for the survey of the 8th US Army installations in Korea, one site in Seoul and one in Taegu. I went by myself a few days before the team arrived to spend some time with my family and met the team at the airport since it was everyone's first trip to Korea.

John was very eager to learn about Korea, even eating lots of garlic trying to please me. I took the team to the Yi-Dynasty Palaces on Saturday and to the Yong-In Folk Village on Sunday along with my sister and brother-in-law. Bob and John dressed up as the old Korean grooms, and they looked pretty goofy, especially John, being so tall, wearing traditional Korean pants that were too short for him.

We used taxi instead of renting a car since nobody wanted to drive in Seoul or Taegu. When I was in a bad mood, John made his go-for buddy Tom sit next to me in the cab. And when I was in a good mood, John sat next to me, breathing . . . Everyone in the cab could hear him breathing as a matter of fact. I couldn't help myself getting turned on, feeling his arms squeezed on me and hearing him breathing, in a tiny Korean taxi.

Panama was the last site scheduled for the survey, and Lt Col Segrest asked me to include him in this survey team. The survey team consisted of Lisa for the network survey, a single guy with ARS for the Honeywell mainframe and application survey, an Army Major to help us around, and myself for the workstations survey. Lt Col Segrest advised me not to have Lisa on this survey team, however, I insisted to have Lisa on this survey team even switching my role for this to accommodate Lisa (network survey had always been my responsibility for other sites).

The Panama site representatives didn't seem to welcome the survey team. The atmosphere was stiff and some of them were questioning us, almost like they were trying to find a reason not to support our project. The DSIA Field Office in Panama summoned Lt Col Segrest as we arrived at the site to question him for not coordinating the visit with them, then had sent out an e-mail to every DSIA Field Offices reprimanding him for breaking the protocol, and that was the bad start.

After the in brief, I went around the building to chat with people along with Lisa, and one of the guys there owned a large boat. "That must be a lot of fun to go out to the ocean every weekend to relax. I wish I could do that," I flattered him. He smiled and invited the survey team to go out to the ocean, with a request that Lisa and I would wear bikinis.

Next morning, Lisa showed up looking like some kind of a Mediterranean Queen. I didn't bring a bikini, and I wore a T-shirt and shorts. As we walked to the boating area, all the cars passing by were honking with drivers waving and whistling. "You too are stopping the Panama traffic!" Lt Col Segrest commented, smiling big.

There were about 30 people who joined this little getaway, and we sailed to a small island. Lisa took off her colorful wrap when we got on the boat, and she had bikini under. She knew how to enjoy her business trip and to excite men! She had been traveling a lot, and I was glad that I asked her to join this survey. Guys kept bugging me that I should wear a bikini. Some guys even tried to drag me to a bikini rental shop, but I was too bashful. I couldn't imagine walking around in a bikini in front of Lt Col Segrest, my task boss, and the guys who I worked with. No way Hosei!!!

Josh, a single guy who was a subcontractor to ARS, Lisa and I were in the same age group, and we hung around together, shopping and exploring different foods. For some nights everyone got together for dinner, and I had the biggest lobster of my lifetime, about 20cm long, for $20, watching the dinner show with Panama folk Dance, which was very enjoyable.

On the last night, Lisa, Josh and I went to the Dance club at the hotel where we were staying. After drinking and dancing for a while, Lisa left, saying she had a book to read. I decided to practice the *Dirty Dancing* with Josh, and that was a mega fun. I didn't know I could do the dirty dancing so well (I only watched the movie). Josh was shocked, very happily. I was the CATCH for the contractor guys, and for him, a subbie, it was like winning a lottery!

Next morning, the Army Major was looking at me differently, a dirty look, whispering something to Lt Col Segrest. This dry naggy-type Major must have come down to the Dance club and saw me dancing. I looked at the

Major guy and shrugged, 'So what'? With that, he shouted, "**We have a disco queen!**" to Lt Col Segrest after giving me a contemptuous look. Lt Col Segrest gave me a quick look, feeling uncomfortable with this Major guy's upset meddling with my personal matter, and nobody talked much after that.

When we returned to the states, Lt Col Segrest thanked me for my hard-work just before we departed at the airport. That was what mattered, get the work done. Work hard and play hard was what I believed in doing, and I tried to make the best of my trip, exploring the new place and have fun as much as I could.

Survey trips were incentive for everyone in the team, and it certainly motivated me to work harder looking forward to the interesting trips!

TURNING INTO A PRO*

When all of the planned surveys were completed, I planned to have a working session with three military services organizations, DISN group, TIP contractors and Mitre representatives to discuss the survey findings. I invited about 30 people for the working session, and it was going to be the biggest meeting that I would host.

On the morning of this meeting, people kept showing up like there was a big conference, filling up the Front Office conference room and standing around for there was no more room. As I was trying to figure out what to do with this unexpected crowd, Mr. Myers asked everyone to go to the conference room downstairs used for all-hands meeting.

Mr. Myers looked at me, apparently very worried about me not being able to handle this situation, when he was giving a short introduction speech as I had asked. After the speech, he just left as if he couldn't bear to watch me getting screwed for having too many people's interest. It was totally over my head, and I sat there thoughtlessly.

Lieutenant Colonel Segrest was the next one to provide the project status, and another Lieutenant Colonel discussed the requirements for remote sites. I was overwhelmed by this turnout, just trying to keep my nerves down, thinking, 'I can only be myself.'

Next was my turn to brief the site connectivity status, and I tried to keep myself in a lower position, speaking in front of the podium like Mr. Myers had done, instead of getting up on the podium. I introduced myself and briefly described the overview of data flow for the TIP networking requirement. I was cooler than cucumber, to my surprise, as I had no idea how I would perform, looking like a very high-speed engineer wearing white neat top with navy strips on shoulder and white pants. In the middle of my introduction speech, Lisa got up and left. She didn't care to watch me shine (probably wished me to screw this so that she could laugh). Bitch!

Everyone was very attentive, surprised and delighted, and Lt Col Segrest shouted in the crowd, "**Chan, get up there!**" smiling ear-to-ear. He looked worried, too, when he was speaking, telling people how it was supposed to be a working meeting trying to cover me. I was performing well beyond his expectation, beyond my own expectation, actually.

I got up onto the podium and presented the survey findings. I had briefing charts prepared to plan the network connectivity needed for the TIP installation, and I asked Bob to switch the slides as I went through them. I had requested Dan to attend this meeting asking him to cover me for technical questions, but he didn't show up, probably mad at me for presenting the connectivity diagrams that he had prepared myself (instead of him). I saw the ARS Program Manager walking out in the middle of my presentation, and about an hour later, Dan showed up, after my briefing was over.

This meeting was planned to discuss the survey findings to correct the survey mistakes and possible connectivity options, but I learned that even the Joint Chiefs of Staff representatives came to this meeting as they were raising questions. Lt Col Segrest covered most of general questions before I had chance to try to come up with the right answers. I knew what I was doing, technically, and I was quicker than I knew myself, covering a few sensitive issues that I didn't have knowledge of, making some guys smile . . .

After my briefing, ARS and Mitre representatives presented possible wide area network connectivity options, and the meeting was over with no complaint from the attendees. I went out with a bunch of guys including Dan to relax and talk about this meeting over a few drinks . . .

Next day, I heard Mr. Myers, Lt Col Segrest, and my Division Manager talking about this meeting, laughing and praising me for being able to handle the meeting that even they would have been scared of.

There were eight sites that did not have an operational LAN, and I worked with three military services representatives to implement the LANs at those sites, which were mostly overseas sites. John brought in another ARS engineer from California, Barbara, an older woman, to help me with the LAN engineering for these eight sites.

An Air Force Major, Barbara, and I went to Remstein Air Force base, then Heidelberg Air Force Base in Germany. We stayed at the military bunker instead of a hotel, and I just walked around the campus in the evening, peeking at a military officer party and playing in a military casino. Some nights three of us went out together and walked on the street to do some shopping, but no weekend to visit other places. It was pretty much all work.

On my return trip, the airport security picked me out for some reason, maybe because I had too many stamps on my passport. I looked at Major Buritt, hoping that he would give me some hint for this airport hassle since he had been stationed in Germany for many years, but he just gave me "chee," his usual "whatever" half-laugh. The airport security took me aside and asked me why I was visiting Germany, and I had to show the DoD travel paperwork to prove that I was there for the US DoD business.

We flew to London to engineer the LAN for a Navy site. DSIA had booked me the first class for this flight, for a change. The cheap government, giving me the economy class for the long flight to Korea and the first class for the shortest flight. Still, better than the economy class for all flights.

I liked London very much, but it was a lonely and dry trip overall. Major Buritt was a dry guy and Barbara was a nagging type woman, not exactly pleasant and rather annoying. I kept thinking about Harry Myers, thinking how nice this trip might have been if I came with him. It makes the world of difference who one travels with . . . I bought some presents for him in London.

When I returned to my office, I went to see Harry Myers to brief him of my trip. "I have a present for you," I said after the short briefing. His face hardened a little, like he was worrying that I was about to bribe him or something uncomfortable was going to happen. I took out a little metal statue of wizard wearing glasses from my jacket pocket and put it onto his table. He smiled big, shyly, looking at the status (not looking at me).

The following week, I flew to Korea with Barbara for the same work. By this trip, she was trying to run me over. She kept bitching about me being there for no reason (she was doing all the work) to one of my customers, Brody, a civilian guy who was responsible for the systems administration there. He made a sarcastic remark about Margarrette Gundersheimer visiting Korea for shopping, and now me, coming for shopping. Barbara was a contractor hired to do this task, and I was there to coordinate the task, to supervise her, my contractor.

While Barbara was gathering information needed to engineer the LAN with Brody, I kept Lt Col Jett a company and talked to other people working there. Lt Col Jett was a sincere Air Force officer, but he always looked lonely, somehow, even though his wife was in Korea with him. I spent many hours sitting next to him in his office, helping him with the PowerPoint charts he was preparing. Some people at the 8th US Army site started referring me as the "Dragon Lady" . . .

Upon the completion of the LAN engineering surveys, I worked with a number of network equipment vendors to evaluate and select the right equipment for the TIP connectivity requirements, negotiating the prices and maintenance services for the equipment. John was developing Site Engineering Plan for the 31 Initial Operational Capability sites for me, and I met frequently with him for that task as well.

TIP project expanded as the Global Communications and Control System (GCCS), and new Program Management Office was established with the Military Officers. A bunch of new military people moved into the OSF building. ACIS and SCC became the primary contractors, and ARS was subcontracted to ACIS. Also a number of small companies were subcontracted to handle various applications added. New contractors moved into the OSF building, and I personally had Dan move into my building. Some people started referring me as the "GCCS Queen" . . .

Dan became my regular lunch mate, and he was pretty proud of being my lunch mate, the power babe! One day, Mr. Harry Myers saw Dan and I going out to lunch together at the parking lot, and Dan waved at Mr. Harry Myers, like he wanted to say, 'I can have lunch with this hot babe, but you can't, can you? ne ne ne ne ne ne~'

60 sites were designated for the GCCS installation, and the new GCCS team needed to survey the added sites and to revisit larger sites. I went to Korea alone this time to survey a few additional smaller facilities. However, when I got there, Lt Col Jett had a list of 22 sites scattered around the country to be surveyed. He had formed a survey team including an Army Captain Smith and a female Navy Lieutenant, Joan, in addition to himself and me. Captain Smith had a pretty Korean wife, and Joan was single.

Four of us hopped 22 sites driving a DSIA Field Office vehicle, starting in Seoul going down to Pusan. I spent the nights at military clubs and slept in the military bunkers with them. At the end of the survey trips, I prepared a report and briefed the 8th US Army representatives. I went to survey two sites for two weeks and ended up staying there for a month and half.

Some other team from another DSIA organization arrived for a different task and asked me to join them, but I was exhausted and wanted to return to America after a month and half in Korea. I needed to return to pay my travel bill, at least. The American Express had tracked me down to Korea and called me at my hotel inquiring about my delinquent payment on the corporate card.

The survey trips to various military installations were an eye-opening experience, and I was becoming very comfortable with myself being able to handle this magnitude of project and what I could accomplish in this environment . . . I got promoted as GS-13 along with Lisa . . .

UNITED NATIONS PROJECT

In the middle of the GCCS site engineering phase, I got selected to support the United Nations project determining the UN Department of Peace Keeping Operations requirements and recommending solutions for modernizing its peacekeeping missions. My new manager, who wasn't exactly fond of me (he was skeptical about me being treated too well for my look), came by my cubicle to tell me that he was very proud of me being selected for this UN task. He had just been promoted as the manager with the reorganization, and he was assigned as my Branch Manager.

A few days later, UN project kick-off meeting hosted by the Project Leader, Bill Stiffler, was held, and I found that he had assigned me as the team leader for the Communications Team. All of my team members were more experienced than me, however, I was the only one with DSIA and the only female member of this team. I was overwhelmed for having to function as the team leader. Apparently, it was a political assignment and I just needed to do my best to coordinate my team's activities.

There were two other teams, Situation Center Analysis team led by another DSIA employee under Bill Stiffler, and the Operations Analysis team led by an old Booz Allen Manager.

My team's responsibility was to analyze UN communications systems and design deployable LAN and communication capabilities for areas with no communications infrastructure available for UN field operations (Rwanda, Somalia, and the likes). The communications team consisted of the best representatives from Aerospace Communications, Booz Allen, Logicons, and SAIC, and I was very pleased with all of my team members. Everyone in my team was very polite and treated me with respect, helping me with directions.

I visited the United Nations for a week, as a member of "Assist Team." Bill asked me and the other two team leaders to attend the meeting with the UN Secretary General (Kofi Annan) and his staff. I was the only minority member from the US side. The atmosphere of this meeting made me nervous. Everyone looked so solemn and uptight. Bill briefed our object of visiting the UN, and everyone seemed very cautious not to make a wrong remark, saying minimum necessary. Mr. Annan's assistant, a young Indian guy, who sat next to Mr. Annan, was wearing tinted glasses in the relatively dark meeting room, looking arrogant, and he talked pompously, sounding like he had the world on his shoulder. Nobody said much except Bill and Mr. Annan's pompous assistant.

After the briefing, the team gathered to plan the interviews with UN personnel. I partnered with Paul, the satellite expert who was with the Aerospace Communications. Paul and I observed the UN communications system operations and interviewed a number of UN personnel.

The first guy we interviewed was a European guy, maybe from Denmark or from Switzerland. His name was Rolf something, clean and sharp looking guy in his 30's, responsible for the satellite system. Maybe he was from Germany or Austria or Netherland, I was trying to guess. He was pretty impressive with impeccable manners and communication skills, and he smiled at me every once a while. He was good looking with different mood than the American guys I was used to, very intriguing.

Bill, two other team leaders and I visited an US Representative who was responsible for the UN field operations, Mr. Lewis. Bill briefed him of our goal for this visit, and Mr. Lewis provided us with some directions, along with organization charts and various documents. It was at the end of the first day there, and Mr. Lewis walked us out of the building. He shook hands with Bill and two other team leaders. Then he paused, looking at me, like he was hesitating to shake hands with me. As I was feeling tiny (not deserving his handshake, looking too young or ???), he extended his hand to me (whew). I smiled like a happy little kid having deserved his handshake, extending my hand, and he put his other hand on my hand, smiling . . .

On the first night, everyone had dinner together at the hotel, drinking and partying, and after that the team members broke down into smaller groups for personal times. I hung around with Bill or Paul mostly. On the weekend, I roamed the Soho market, buying a bunch of little things I really didn't need. Paul took me to a Polish restaurant, and I took him to a Korean restaurant. Bill was under some medication, reluctant to try any new dishes. Paul had lived in Indonesia for two years, and he seemed very comfortable hanging around with me despite the age difference. And I was actually more comfortable with Paul than other younger members of my team, who were too much like guys.

Participation and cooperation by UN personnel were very high. Paul and I interviewed various UN personnel responsible for different parts of the satellite communication systems and some administrative workers to understand their operations and missions. Tom Baxter, Zoltan Nagy, Hiroo Takeuchi, Bill Scheiber . . . I piled up my business card collections there.

The three teams planned to collaborate with each team's study and write a report proposing solutions for modernizing the UN peacekeeping missions, including interoperability with GCCS and other U.S. military resources. I coordinated meetings to discuss and incorporate what each of my team members had put together and what to do next. In addition, I prepared the GCCS and other military C3 systems infrastructure for the Communication Team Report.

Unfortunately, I had to drop out of this team before we completed the report. I needed to go to Hawaii and Korea for the GCCS installation coordination meetings. The GCCS project had higher priority. My UN project team members joked, "Tough call!"

I felt very lucky to be a part of this once in a lifetime experience, another eye-opening experience for the international organization.

DRIVING 76 MILES AN HOUR . . .

Lieutenant General Brown, DSIA Director, was scheduled to visit the OSF building, and Mike asked me to wait for him at the lab. LTG Brown was Black, Air Force, quite distinguishing looking. The six stars on his shoulders made me nervous since it was the first time for me to brief a military General, with no practice with one or two star Generals. I explained how the equipment in the lab were used for the GCCS testing and briefed him what I had learned from three beta site installations. He asked a few questions, looking into my eyes, and I answered his questions, looking into his eyes. Someone told me I was hard to read. He was hard to read.

The team revised the installation procedures based on the experience at three beta sites, and I formed four fielding teams, with myself leading the fielding at the Pacific sites including Korea. Each team consisted of a government team leader, a network engineer, UNIX server expert(s), a PC expert, and US military operations expert(s). I had the scum-ball contractor Dan on my team, the best network engineer.

Dan and I went to Hawaii to prepare the sites for the GCCS fielding, and from Hawaii, we flew to Korea. It was the first Korea trip for Dan, and I took him to the Kyeong-Bok Palace where the Yi Dynasty prospered for 500 years and to other small palaces. Dan had no problem with Korean foods, kimchi and other spicy foods, eager to try whatever I recommended. We drank everyday and walked around the Itaewon shopping district almost every day, buying small souvenirs.

On Friday afternoon, we had work accomplished early and headed to a bar. We drank beers all afternoon at a dimly lighted bar. When we came out to the street, I felt like kissing him. So I did, in the middle of the streets. That was a very unusual thing to do, for Koreans, and even for me, kissing in the bright day light, to a White guy, in Korea. Dan was a pretty reserved and well-behaved guy, too. Until then, I didn't think he was my type, just thought he was a very reliable guy.

We met at a Ruby Tuesday for lunch a few days after returning to the states.

"Hey, how are you?"
"Oh, I am doing fine. Are you all recovered from the trip?"
"Yea, pretty much back to normal now." He smiled shyly, "So, what are we going to do now?"
"What are we going to do? Nothing, whatever happens happens . . . "
"Okay, I like that."
"Were you afraid that you would have to marry me now or something?"
"Ha Ha~ No, I was just wondering if I should treat you differently. I had never done anything like that since I married Pat."
"I didn't think you were the kind of guy who fooled around. I had fun, and that's all there is to it. I wouldn't mind doing it again."
"I enjoyed the trip very much. Friends?"
"Friends!"

Dan had ordered scotch & water and I ordered whisky sour. We cheered and sipped the drinks a little. Neither talked for a few minutes, thinking about what happened in Korea, feeling a little shy meeting in a normal environment.

"What you looked like sitting on the bed got indented in my head."

"How is Debbie?"

"Oh, she is fine."

"You still have feelings for her, right?"

"Yea, I like her. I like her a lot, but she is kinda like a sister."

"Would she approve of what you did with me?"

"No, she will be very upset if she finds out."

"She is not interested having sex with you, so why would it bother her? She should allow you to have what you like to do or need to do? But I guess it wouldn't be the best thing to do to sing a song about . . ."

"Ha ha~, no, I wouldn't do that to her. She is upset about her body changing and doing some exercise these days."

"I see. I have a friend who lost interest in sex since she was about 30. She told me that she was having sex with her husband once a month or something like that."

"That's too bad. Debbie and I were good for first two years, and after that, it got slowed down, and now, it's more like once in every six months, for five minutes, hweek! done."

"Ha ha~ That's no fun. I need more than five minutes."

"Ha ha~ I bet you can handle a few hours easily. I may need to start taking something to keep up with you!"

"Snakes are good, oysters are good, too. I heard some rich Korean guys drinking fresh blood out of deer horn. Yuk!"

"I wouldn't go that far. I like oysters. Do you like oysters? We can get some oysters next time if you want."

"Yea, I do, as a matter of fact. That sounds good."

John left ARS and joined the DSIA to continue to support the TIP/GCCS task. He was on probation for a sexual harassment and had been off the project because Lisa and an ARS female complained about his behavior during a survey trip. He joined the DSIA to travel the world around with me, he said. In any case, I was glad to have him around . . .

A young Lieutenant came to my cubicle and asked me to accompany him for a site survey, an Air Force site in Colorado. I was busy with TIP initial operations sites and declined his request. To my surprise, he got down on his knees, begging me, "I heard you are the best, please, please." My boss happened to walk by, saw what this young Lieutenant was doing, surprised by this young guy's playful over-gesture (and my popularity or importance maybe), and said, "Chan, you've got to help him," smiling. I had to agree to accompany him for his survey, of course.

Dan and I had another trip to Hawaii and Korea for GCCS installation. This time, for two months, one month in Hawaii and one month in Korea . . . At each site, I briefed customers on our fielding plan and asked the customers to install the GCCS applications with the fielding team overlooking and helping them if/when they ran into problems. The customers were very satisfied with this approach. Every morning, I briefed the customers reporting the progress and installation issues and sent the Installation Status Report to the DSIA GCCS PMO back in Washington DC every day.

When the CIPRNET router and the interface (premise router) were installed and configured, I sent the Installation Status Report to the GCCS PMO over the CIPRNET to share the exciting moment of a new network coming alive.

Dan left early from the Korea installation trip, as soon as he completed his task. A few days later, I had a problem of the site network administrator deleting the password of the CIPRNET Hub Router that Dan had configured. It was new to all of us, and I obtained the password recovery procedures and coordinated the recovery of the Hub Router in Taegu with the CIPRNET engineer in Hawaii. I was in Seoul, and Lt Col Jett flew me down to Taegu in a 7-seater Air-force plane. The ride was pretty rough, soaring and plunging and shaking. Maybe it was due to the Captain who wasn't one of the better pilots flying the plane or just because the plane was small, maybe both. I felt some nausea in my stomach, but it was exciting, almost like riding a rollercoaster.

I had two hours to recover the password and reconfigure the hub router. After I had recovered the password, I called Dan. It was after the midnight in America and he was in his deep sleep. He woke up quickly and helped me configure the router. He was darn good, just woke up from the deep sleep but not a little detail skipped his mind, even waiting for me to complete all of the tests to make sure that everything was working properly. His professional alert impressed me, and when I returned from this installation trip, I wrote a formal appreciation note for Dan.

Soon after I completed the GCCS V1.0 installations, I took some time off to visit my sister's family in Paris. My professional life was wonderful, and everyone envied me for flying around the world. I traveled around the France for three weeks with my sister's family riding and test-driving my brother-in-law's Mercedes-Benz.

My next task, which I assigned to myself, was to coordinate and develop GCCS network and system management systems. I had the GCCS project, and everything related to this project was pretty much up to me by this time. Some people thought I was being too much by this time, too, hoping that I would go away and give them a new chance. An older woman actually came by my cubicle just to say, "Someone like you should work for a private company. Someone like me need to work here."

Upon completion of the Concept of Operation development for the GCCS network management I decided to explore some other opportunities with private industry before I turned into one of those lazy government employees hiding in their cubicles with nobody knowing what they were doing. I took a position with a network consulting firm in Atlanta, GA.

PART 2
ADVENTURE TO SOUTHERN STATES

WORKING AS NETWORK DESIGN CONSULTANT

During one of my trips to Atlanta, I met a guy, Carl Troxel, an Army Major, who was responsible for a small Army site in Atlanta. He had become my date, a long distance date, and soon after he retired from the Army and got a job with BNS as a Managing Consultant. Carl was more than confident that I would be a good fit there, persuading the HR manager to bring me in. With his persistence, the woman HR manager called me on a *Sunday evening* to arrange an interview.

My boss-to-be, Barry Koch, was impressed with me during the interview as I got up and drew the diagrams of the network describing my DoD networking experience. Carl was present at my interview, and he looked very proud of me conducting the interview like a pro, proud that he recommended me as a networking expert.

The first day I joined the group, Carl came to me with a proposal that needed to be submitted to the potential customer next day, and it was missing the bill of materials. That was a bit much. I needed to learn the customer requirements, checked the available/operable devices and all. He said, "Sorry to have to put you in this situation, but I can't find anyone who can do this right now. Just do what you can, please." It appeared to me that he needed me there more than I needed him to help me in. Maybe that was why he had pushed the less than enthusiastic HR hard to bring me in quickly.

I quickly reviewed the document and specified the bill of materials, with nervous Carl watching and waiting as the closing time approached. Just as I was completing the task, he called his customer, informing that he would be about an hour late for submitting his proposal. Talking about quick and dirty solution, probably sloppy, too, but that was the best I could do for this situation. We drove to the building where the customer was waiting, waiting to receive the proposal, put some stamp on and go home.

Carl won the project. He was so thrilled when he got the news that he ran to me and gave me a big hug. I was a new *star* and immediately, I was assigned to work on a troubled task to write a technology migration strategy document for the Dorchester School District including network architecture, hardware requirements, operating systems, databases, possible educational applications as well as the implementation plan.

This work required broad technical knowledge and to do research on the emerging technologies. Someone, a former Booz Allen consultant, had started this task and quit having trouble with her Managing Consultant, unclear guidance or whatever reason unknown. And no one was able to continue or interested in picking up this work.

Much of the technology research had been done, written randomly, which was confusing at first. I created a Table of Content and sorted the writings, adding missing information. The disordered and confusing bunch of information started to look like an understandable, organized document. To meet the deadline, I put 60 hours a week, working on weekends and sometimes all night long. One of the VP's, who had been responsible for this task, supplemented some areas where my knowledge was short, working late at the office with me, eating pizza. Then he presented the completed document to his customer.

For this work, I was praised for my excellent contribution at an all-hands meeting, and I received 10% increase in my salary. I was pretty proud of myself for pulling this task and felt great about my new job, felt great about management and co-workers as well, for encouraging and even rewarding me more than I had expected for this work. I had thought my starting salary was rather low, just $2000/year more than what I had earned at DSIA, but I didn't expect any kind of salary increase so quickly, within a few months. The president of the company even gave me a special birthday card, and the woman HR manager who seemed reluctant to bring me in asked me to serve as a member of their Employee Opinion Forum. I had become a flying- star for this work.

After a few months, I lost interest in Carl and became interested in another single guy, Terry, who happened to be Carl's boss, one of the three VP's there. Terry seemed like a very solid and straightforward guy, the opposite of Carl in many ways (trustable vs. not trustable for one). Both of them had just hit the over-the-hill 40's, eligible bachelors. They seemed to dislike each other personally, but they were fine professionally.

Terry was compassionate and supportive of me dealing with some southerners who weren't very thrilled with me, trying to pick on me and even trying to gang people against me. I was the only Asian in this group, and there was only one Black guy. Terry reprimanded me when I made a mistake, with good intention, wishing me to do better, instead of complaining or making a negative comment to someone else, like most others would do, just being judgmental.

When some people tried to gang up against me, some of those who were friendly to me became unreliable all of a sudden, trying to go with the flow. Terry always firmly stood by me, and I thought he was tough and had the backbone, solid as rock. He was good-looking, too, with trustable eyes and perfect body.

The VP who helped me writing the Dorchester School District technology planning document, Greg, often stopped by my cubicle to joke around, but he was one of those who switched his position quickly, always going with the flow. He was very judgmental and joked to others about me when some people said something negative about me, telling them what they wanted to hear. He was married, somewhat older than Terry, probably in his late 40's.

Carl was the Managing Consultant for the Government and Education vertical market, and for his big $800 million proposal, he selected me as the technical lead. I worked with Greg and a junior consultant, along with some vendors providing various devices. I was responsible for network design and writing most part of the proposal, and Greg helped me with video network that I had little knowledge of.

For the presentation to the customer, Carl was the briefer, and both Terry and Greg attended the presentation since it was one of the largest bids, bidding against IBM and other large systems integrators. I was nervous about having to cover all of the technical aspects of this proposal.

I had stretched far beyond my previous design experience, and the best thing I could do was to look confident, and to figure the exact solutions (with trial and error) when we got the project. I just hoped that the customers wouldn't be able to ask me to clarify any technical details, and they didn't.

I wore a dark green double breast jacket with a light green blouse with muted geometric patterns and a slightly flared stone-color pants. It was my high professional look those days. As I was coming out of the building after the briefing, Terry was taking off in his car and he stared at me for a few seconds. He hadn't looked at me like that before. My dress-up style must have impressed him, like it did Mr. United Nations, what was his name, who smiled with his eyes.

It was a young group, and most people were new: 90% White males, a few females, and a Black guy, Paul, who was my closest friend there. Paul generated a nice and warm mood, and whenever I felt like taking a break, I visited his cubicle to talk to him. He always welcomed me with a big, nice smile. Several new consultants were hired after I joined the group, and one of them was a Southern bitch named Leslie. She was good-looking wearing tight jeans to work, but she looked rather wicked, reminding me of a snake with deep, slanted eyes.

For one of the proposals, Leslie and I were on the same team, and I learned that she had absolutely no technical skill. She was a former accountant! She was the same level consultant with me, but I had to do all of the technical work, from designing network to specifying the bill of materials, to writing the proposal. While I was pulling my hair out trying to come up with solutions, she was just flirting with guys . . . I asked her to edit the document before we submitted it to the Document Group since she couldn't do anything else. And she was having trouble doing that, too, bitching and cursing while she was trying to format the document. I just rolled my eyes listening to her cursing at the computer systems. Another new junior consultant, Larry, was on my team for this task, helping me with networking devices.

Three of us went to Charleston, South Carolina, to visit customers. I had to stay overnight to collect necessary information, and I asked a girl with my apartment management office to look after my beloved dog Tundra for one evening, to feed her and let her out before going to bed. I drove to Charleston and checked into a motel. Leslie and Larry were already there, and Larry was sitting outside smoking a cigar, looking ridiculous. I looked at him, raising my brows, and asked him, "You smoke cigar?" He smiled repulsively and said, "I only do when I am on a trip." He had some strange stupid pompous expression on his face. It must be the cigar making him do that, a self-indulged feeling like a big-shot satisfaction of some kind.

Leslie was from Charleston, and we went to a restaurant for dinner, ordered shrimp and lobster, as she suggested. She flirted with the waiter, too. She was living with a guy, her boyfriend, but she flirted with every guy at the office. She must be considering her behaviors as some kind of southern charm . . . . After the dinner, Leslie and Larry were heading to a bar for drinks, and I declined to join them feeling that I was the extra and came back to my motel.

Next morning, I met with them to visit the customer, and they were looking at each other meaningfully. Obviously, they slept together after the drink. I was somewhat surprised by her carefreeness with this young scumish guy who was younger and lower level than herself, but none of my business. The discouraging part of this trip was that I was the lead engineer asking questions and networking information to customers, but the customers always provided answers and documents I asked for to Larry, trying to belittle me. Leslie just flirted with them.

The HR arranged Happy Hour on every Friday evening, and I was one of the regulars going to this Happy Hour. Greg and Carl were always there as well. Terry came every other week, and when he did, I stayed for hours, until the end, usually getting drunk (getting a bit more relaxed, that is). I was never one of those who seemed to lose their mind when they were drunk. My mind was always pretty clear no matter how much I drank. I became more relaxed and talkative after I had a few drinks, and I liked to hang around Terry, liked to see him outside of the office.

My professional confidence level increased significantly working as a consultant, charging customers $150 an hour (although my salary was based on making $35 an hour). When I needed to perform a task at a customer's facility, it made me nervous to think that the customer would expect me to perform $150/hour skills. Nevertheless, it motivated me to stay sharp and improve myself to meet customer's expectation.

One day, Terry saw me going out to lunch, and I had a suede jacket on, with my tiger muffler. His eyes lighted, and he stared at me with deep guy's eyes. He looked great in a leather bomber jacket. He certainly had some wild streak about him, very trustable at the same time. He kept me happy and motivated to do well there.

'Nothing risked, nothing gained.' What to risk (and what not to risk) would depend on many factors such as one's values and goals, and I thought it was worth risking my stable job to explore a new challenge, for a better option that I might be missing . . . ?

COMPUTER SYSTEM NOT WORKING!

I needed to get my car inspected, and every gas station where I stopped by had a problem of their computer system not working. One of the gas stations I went, one guy said, "I will do that for you," looking at me up and down, like he was about to do me a big favor. He asked another guy who actually performed the inspection working on a car in the garage, "Can you do the inspection now?" and the guy in the garage snapped at the first guy, "Don't you know that our computer system is broken?!"

Discouraged by these gas stations, I delayed getting my car inspected and registering it in the Georgia state. On one Sunday, a cop pulled me over. "Your registration is two months overdue. Can I see your driver's license and the registration card?" "Oh, is it? I didn't realize." I tried to play a dumb female driver and gave him my Virginia driver's license and the old Virginia state registration.

The cop walked over to his patrol car and came back after a few minutes, with a wicked smile and told me to step out of my car. I actually had no idea why I needed to step out of my car and looked at him, puzzled. Delayed registration shouldn't be a crime to step out of the car, I was thinking, and he shouted, "**Step out of your car!**" I stepped out of my car, and he told me to get into his patrol car, saying, "Your driver's license has been suspended, and you are under arrest!"

Oh, shoot! I remembered getting a reckless driving ticket on Rt. 95, in North Carolina, driving 95 miles an hour, when I was driving back and forth between Virginia and Georgia. I had just bought a brand new Nissan Maxima, and I was testing the performance of my new car with my first long distance driving. And I forgot about the speeding ticket all together in the midst of moving down to Georgia.

The cop had my car towed away, and he drove me to his police station. At the police station, he searched my body for some kind of weapon, having me standing against the wall. That felt like a criminal. I was traffic criminal. Another cop who was friendlier and seemed compassionate of me said I could go home paying the bailout. I didn't have enough cash on me and asked him if I could pay it with my personal check. "No, cash only," he said. I needed to call someone to bail me out, and the only number I could remember was Carl's home number.

"Hello."
"Carl, this is Chan. Sorry to have to bother you at this hour, but I am in trouble and I need your help."
"What is it?" He didn't sound thrilled.
"I got arrested for driving with the suspended license, and I am at a police station. I need you to bring me $200 now. Can you please do that?"
"What?! I don't believe this! You got arrested?"
"Yes, I got arrested! I will tell you what happened later, but I need you to bring $200 to get out of here, please!"
"Sigh-. Where are you? Give me the address of the police station."

Two hours later, Carl showed up and paid the fine. He was in no mood to be friendly to me, didn't say a word, and gave me a contemptuous look. He drove me to my apartment, not happily, and asked me not to bother him with this kind of trouble again telling me that I was causing a trouble for his new marriage. He had just married to his old Korean girlfriend, and she was all upset, he said. I regretted moving down to this stupid new area and said, "Sorry, I didn't have a choice."

Carl and his wife came to my apartment next morning to help me get my car back. He must have brought her to prove to her that he was just helping an old friend who was new to the area. She looked sick and she wasn't saying anything. I tried to be friendly with her, but she didn't seem comfortable talking with me, probably intimidated by my professionalism and English communication skills. Carl had told me that he had trouble communicating with her, and that was one of the reasons why he was drawn to me, for being able to talk.

I got my car back, but I couldn't drive until I cleared my driver's license. I called Terry and told him about my situation, and he arranged one of the consultants who lived nearby me to pick me up next morning. As soon as I arrived at the office, I went to see Terry. He looked at me with somewhat dissatisfied eyes for the first time.

"Don't call Carl, call me if you run into a problem like this."
"I didn't have your number or anyone's number, and Carl's home number was the only number I memorized in this area. Did he say something to you?"
"Yes, he complained to me that he got into trouble with his wife because you called him."

"I see. His wife came to my apartment with him yesterday to help me get my car back, and she didn't seem upset. I kinda knew her, she is a Korean. Anyway, I didn't have a choice, but it won't happen again."

"Okay."

Jeff, a good looking young marketing guy, came by to tease me, "So, you got busted, huh, Ha ha ha~" He seemed to think that I, seemingly a naïve and polite foreign-born, had just become a more interesting person, all excited about me getting a speeding ticket and even getting busted! He started calling me "jail bird."

I had to register my car as quickly as possible, and I asked Paul to drive me to the DMV. He was more than willing to help, such a nice guy. The DMV always seemed to be full of low-life looking people and Paul looked out of the place, looking like a professional, but he was smiling and being friendly to strangers, chatting with some people sitting around, waiting . . . That was why I liked him, he treated everyone with good heart.

I asked Jeff to come along with me when I had to visit a middle school for a survey. He followed my car in his blue truck. It somewhat surprised me to see this sleek guy with a pretty face driving a truck, however, he looked sexy driving a truck, somehow. After following me for a while, he changed the lane driving past me. I tried to follow him for a few minutes, and he kept increasing the speed. Men! I gave up, I didn't need to get another speeding ticket right after I had gone through a trouble for, and that was probably why he was speeding up (going 'I can do this, but you can't, can you?').

While I was doing the survey, taking notes on the systems used, Jeff talked to customers. After the survey, Jeff and I stopped at a bar. He looked so sexy that I thought about inviting him to my apartment after several drinks. Then I thought about Terry and decided I'd better not.

My adventure to Georgia turned out to be a bad move, after all. I had difficulties dealing with southern customers for one. And personally, I felt like I was living in a cage, afraid to go out for a long drive on weekends, afraid of getting lost and running into bad racists at some remote area (the possibility of getting lynched actually popped into my head). Through my experience in Georgia, I learned my lesson how important it was to choose a right place, both professionally and personally.

TERRY YOUNG

The president of BNS and three VP's were scheduled to make speeches at the all-hands New Year Planning meeting. This women president treated me well, and one day, she said to me, "It's true, it's lonely at the top." I liked her. I thought she was cool, the most successful woman professional in the engineering field who I had chance to meet so far. She was single, too.

I was sitting with Paul, and Terry was the second speaker. It was the first time I had seen Terry speaking in front of everyone, and he was a terrific speaker! What was really toughing was that it looked like what he cared most was me, kept looking at me sitting as an audience watching him shine.

One day, I wont to work very early, around 7 o'clock, and ran into Terry in front of the elevator. As we walked into the office, a junior consultant looked at Terry, then at me, with suspecting eyes. Terry took a different path, walking around the cubicle, to reach his office. As more people came in to the office, some people started gossiping about Terry and me spending the night together. Geez. I thought it was rather unnecessary that Terry took a longer path to reach his office, but it took no time to learn why. It didn't bother me, but he had to be more careful trying to prevent this kind of office gossip for his position, obviously.

Except Terry, I started to regret my move to Georgia. I had seen enough of repellent southern attitude towards me, and I'd be much better off moving back to Washington DC area, no doubt. Luckily, I got a job offer from Karlmon Dietech, and my experience working as a networking consultant was a big plus for landing that job. So it wasn't just a bad move.

The night before I moved back to Washington DC, I called Terry to say good-bye.

"Hi Terry, this is Chan."
"Hi Chan."
"I am moving back to Virginia tomorrow. Everything's packed, and the movers will pick up my stuffs tomorrow morning."
"............."
"I like to see you before I go."
"Can you come to my house?"
"Sure, what's the address?"
"1403 Dunwood Crossing."
"Okay, see you in about an hour or so."
"Okay."

It took me almost two hours to find his house. My sense of direction had always been pretty bad, and it was dark when I left my apartment. His house was located in a very quiet residential area, and it was a relatively small single house. I took a deep breath and knocked on his door.

"Hi" I said, smiling. "Come on in," Terry said, smiling. He didn't seem exactly comfortable, probably a little nervous, as I was. "Do you want to see the house?" He asked, and I said, "Sure."

We quickly walked around the house, living room, dining room, and kitchen on the first floor and three bedrooms upstairs. No decoration whatsoever, with a computer in the dining room and books piled up on every table. Definitely unorganized. "How long have you lived in this house?" I asked looking at boxes cluttered everywhere. "I've lived here for about a year and half." 'Single guys must take a long time to unpack moving boxes' I was wondering and said, "So, this is what the single guy's house looks like, huh, messy with things not in place."

Terry sat on the sofa, and I sat next to him.

"Why did you want to see me?"
"I don't know, I just did."
"Can I get you something to drink?"
"Sure, what you got?"
"I have some beers, whisky, might have some other liquors."
"Can you make some whisky sours?"
"No, I just have whisky."
"Okay, beer is good."

We walked over to the kitchen, and he opened the refrigerator to get some beers for both of us. There were barely any foods in his refrigerator, just full of beers.

"What would be doing with your new job?"

"I'll be supporting an Army project, doing the network engineering. It's a project migrating the IBM mainframe systems into the client-server architecture with TCP/IP network. I worked on a similar project before, so it would be good."

"Sounds like a good job."

"I think so, I got lucky, I guess. What would you be doing when the BNS gets merged into BSC?"

"I don't know yet. I could join BSC, I suppose, but I am thinking about looking for some other opportunities, possibly with the Allied Communications."

"Any chance moving to Washington DC area?"

"I lived in Washington DC for 9 years. DC is too busy and too crazy for my taste."

"Why? What made you move down to Atlanta?"

"I got convicted for felony, and I was in prison for eight months."

"Really? Or are you trying to scare me?"

"Really, and I know I am not missing anything in DC."

"What kind of felony?"

"It was some industry felony. It's a long story and I'd rather not talk about that right now."

"Okay. I guess Atlanta is good. It's a new high-tech city, but I don't think I fit well in the southern states. They just are not used to dealing with somebody like me, I guess. I even had trouble getting my stupid car inspected, you know. So many gas stations have some kind of computer problem. I think their computers work just fine until I walk into their gas stations."

"Ha ha~ I imagine you would have some difficulties around here . . . What do you like to do?"

"What do I like to do? "

"I am pretty wild, probably too wild for you."

"How is that? I am adventurous, I think. Tell me why you would be too wild for me."

"I am into the deep throat."

"Deep throat?"

"Yes, have you ever done that?"

"No, thought deep throat was somebody's nickname, associated with Nickson thing or something."

"Ha Ha~ I would marry you if you do deep throat. I thought about marrying a woman once for that."

"Really? Why didn't you marry her, whoever she was?"

"She was a married woman, and her husband was sick, had a cancer. I waited for her to settle the situation for two years, but she said she just couldn't leave her sick husband. She got me into it, and I've been looking for a woman who would enjoy doing that. Once you get used to that, there is nothing like it. It's a total ecstasy."

"Is it? I can't even imagine. I would think woman will have trouble breathing or something?"

"You will gag, and your eyes will become watery."

"...................."

"You are very cute, but you seemed pretty naïve."

"I am naïve, I guess, I grew up in Korea and I am still learning the American ways, so. What kind of woman do you like, besides doing the deep throat thing?"

"What I like is to have someone waiting for me in a very short skirt and a low-cut top. I will take you out to a restaurant if you wear clothes like that. I want everyone in the restaurant to know that you were going to be fucked by me right after the dinner. And after the dinner, I am going to fuck you at the parking lot."

"Sounds interesting, but I've never done anything like that, not sure if I would be comfortable. "

"That's the kind of things I like to do with you. You look like a playboy's dream girl, very sexy. You make me want to be naughty."

"Do I? I like to play, but I am not the playboy bunny girl type."

"I want you to be the bunny girl wearing a collar."

"I will make a terrible bunny girl, even if I try."

"You might enjoy once you try. Another thing I like to do is to go to the Victoria's Secret with you, and fuck you in the back room while you are trying those lingerie on."

"There are other people in the back room. It's just like a cubicle with doors."

"So what! When you are outrageous, others will run away. They will be embarrassed to watch me fuck you in there."

"I never thought of doing things like that. Do you think about sex?"

"Oh, I think about sex all the time, even when I am working, all day long, 8 hours a day."

"Oh, geez ...... You know I like you, I even thought about how good it would be to be your wife."

"I think you are infatuated by me, I've been infatuated before."

"I don't know if I am infatuated, I just like you a lot."

He put his arms around me, and I lifted my eyes to look into his eyes. He kissed me, and he felt like he was burning. I was warm, but I didn't feel hot. I liked him a lot, and I even thought about how trustable he would be as a husband. I told him once when I was drunk after the Company Happy Hour that I would be proud to be his wife, making him laugh. He didn't take me seriously at that time, of course. I was half-serious and half-drunk.

Terry wasn't exactly happy with my lukewarm response and told me that I wasn't being honest with myself. I thought I was, but my body wasn't cooperating with my mind. In any case, he was good enough for both of us, playing with my mind, telling me stories for me to imagine all night long. He was a very trustable guy, frank and straightforward, and even good-looking with great body. He said I was very intriguing, but I was too naïve for his taste, I figured.

It was an interesting night, very different, and that was the last time I saw Terry.

PART 3
SUMMER TIME

It took two weeks for Alex to go through the process for me to join his group. He broke all the rules to bring me in as fast as possible, he told me . . . Under the normal circumstance it would have taken 2-3 months.

Alex was one of the on-site SCC contractors who worked on the GCCS system and network management plan. I didn't know Alex personally, just remembered that he looked like a smart guy with sparkling eyes and good leadership when Dan told me about this job. Alex had contacted Dan for this job, but Dan accepted another position and passed it onto me as the next candidate.

The SBIS project was similar to the GCCS, transitioning the mainframe-oriented operating environment into the TCP/IP network-based client-server architecture. The differences were that the SBIS was to migrate the IBM mainframe (unclassified operating environment), whereas the GCCS was to migrate the Honeywell mainframe (classified), and the Army project vs. Joint project. The SBIS project was less complicated with the backbone network already in place, being operational.

Alex assigned me to work with another network engineer, Fred, who was the only Karlmon Dietech network engineer (and the only Black engineer there). Fred seemed pretty happy to have me working with him and introduced me to his contractor, Don, who was doing most of the hands-on configuration of the networking devices. Don was very technical and knowledgeable, and he helped me getting familiar with all the devices in the lab. Three of us got along very well, meeting with networking vendors, developing new engineering requirements, and upgrading the testing equipment in the lab.

About a week after I joined the group, Alex asked me to come to the Program Manager's office located across the street. I got there a few minutes late, almost out of breath, running across the street. "Sorry, I was in a meeting," I said, looking at Alex. He looked a bit embarrassed for my being late for the first meeting with the Big Boss, and said "She is working," making an awkward smile at the Big Boss.

Holy Smoke! He was GORGEOUS! Alex introduced me to him saying that I was an Electrical Engineering major. The gorgeous program manager said he majored Chemical Engineering and smiled meaningfully, thinking about something for a few second. He probably majored the Chemical Engineering because the starting salary for the Chemical Engineering was the highest, I thought. I learned that when I was graduating as the Electrical Engineering major, that the Chemical Engineering major had slightly higher starting salary than the Electrical Engineering major. I thought that was why he was smiling anyway. He talked briefly about the SBIS program and welcomed us, me and another new guy on board. There were a lot of good-looking guys in the Engineering group, and after seeing Da BOSS, I felt like I hit a home-run!

Steve Thompson, Alex's boss, hosted project status meeting once a week. At the first meeting I attended, I was sitting quietly, listening, trying to get some feel for the project. There was the lead engineer of the group, Tom, and he was doing all the talking. It was the first time I had seen Tom. Nobody had introduced me to him for some reason. He was brilliant and good-looking! And he kept looking at me, joyfully. Others seemed pretty confused about the project and I burst into laugh, and I was laughing like crazy that I had to cover my face with my notebook.

Everyone became very quiet, and Mr. Thompson was getting annoyed by my ridiculous long laugh. Luckily, Tom laughed with me, Ha Ha Ha~ He was more like laughing at me laughing like crazy! I cleared my voice to control myself. Steve Thompson seemed to be puzzled what made me laugh so uncontrollably, but he continued meeting without saying anything to me. Then a few minutes later, I had to laugh again, briefly this time, had to get the leftover-laugh out of my system. Tom laughed too, looking at me bursting out the leftover-laugh.

The secretary came in to the meeting room and gave me my first pay-check, no one else. I felt a little guilty receiving the paycheck by myself. I had no idea why she brought in just my paycheck to the meeting, why she couldn't wait until the meeting was over. In any case, Tom said, "Great! Your first paycheck!" From then on, Tom became my best friend there.

This group used to be the MBI Federal Systems Sector and recently merged into the Karlmon Dietech Systems Integration Sector, and they were still using the old MBI mainframe systems including the e-mail system that was difficult to use. I was trying to write my first e-mail to Alex and Tom about some issues and became irritated by the difficulty of correcting my typing mistakes or making some changes.

I needed to let them know that this old e-mail system was a pain to use: *"ps: when are we going to change this early 19 century e-mail system to Microsoft or Lotus?"* I walked over to Alex's office to check if he received my e-mail since it was my first e-mail there. Tom's office was nearby, and he was laughing like crazy, Kee Kee Kee Kee Kee . . . . Then Tom came over and said, "early 19 century? Ha Ha Ha~" When he returned to his office, I heard guys going into his office and laughing about my email.

A few months later, Fred learned that I was a higher level than him when everyone received business cards. All of a sudden, he changed his attitude towards me, unwilling to cooperate with me and even trying to avoid me. He went around telling other lower-level people about my level. Then he went to see Alex to dispute my and his levels. Alex asked me to come to his office and explained to Fred why I was the higher level, and I would be taking more responsibility soon. I talked to Fred about my previous experience as a network engineer, leading the GCCS network engineering and working as a consultant for the network consulting firm, but Fred was still upset, unwilling to work with me.

So, I started to work more closely with Doug, who was with TA&T, a single guy with a sharp tongue. He was a contractor supporting the networking task, but he was more like a consultant having much more experience than me or Fred. Fred was one of the uglier guys there with freckles all over his face, and Doug commented, "Fred doesn't count, his gun's not turned on . . . " And everybody laughed. It was 90% male engineering group, and most guys there were pretty delighted to have me around, eyes lighting up and smiling when I visited their cubicles with questions or some work-related issues . . . Tom and Doug were two guys who I worked closely with, after spending a few months with Fred.

Tom was sitting in Alex's office when I walked over to Alex's office. I stood at the door asking Alex, "How do we clear the ECP?" Before Alex answered my question, Tom commented, "Female engineers! They don't know what they are doing." I crumpled a little sticker paper happened to be in my hand into a ball and threw it at Tom's head. He raised his hand and blocked the tiny ball perfectly, without looking, his eyes still on Alex. "Nice block!" Alex said, watching us and laughing.

One who I had trouble with was a female engineer, Jennifer Mott. She had been a secretary for 18 years for this company, then she had some technical training to become an Associate, and she was administering the NT network for this group. She didn't like me from the moment I walked in and kept deleting my user-id from the system. She looked like a tough bitch, not pretty but loose, showing up to work wearing sleepwear-like clothes . . . Apparently she had been playing the babe for the group with the user-id *"babe,"* and my presence was making her nervous. She was pushy and obnoxious, often saying, "It's **my** company" when I was around her.

I felt lucky to be with this group and felt sorry for the guys working there. So many good-looking guys, and just this one babe, an unattractive harsh bitch-ish female with big mouth. She was a divorcee with a daughter, and she kept bitching about me not doing my share of work for the group, making everyone else pay for me. Some guys got tired of her bitching about me and giving me hard time, and they started to refer her name as Jennifer *Moth*.

One evening, after most people had left, Doug came to chat with me . . . He sat on the floor with his back against the cubicle across my cubicle and we were just carrying on small talks; how I felt about the place, tasks, and things. I said, "I am barely surviving," trying to be modest, and he responded, "There's a fine difference between surviving and being dragged on . . . " What?? Did he mean that I was being dragged on by him or something??

I knew that the group had an evaluation meeting of me, after I was there for three months, and Doug was the strongest supporter of me, I learned, having worked closely with me as another network engineer. Everyone liked him better than any Karlmon Dietech engineers. He was a very reasonable and cool guy. I must have been under-performing their expectation of me, or Alex had been babying me not assigning me more difficult task. Actually, the core network engineering had been completed when I joined the group, and that was why the lead network engineer had left this group.

I didn't go to work for two days, wondering whether I should quit and find another job. I called Tom to let him know that I would be out of the office to take care of some personal matters. We talked for a while and he said something about "falling in love for some reason." I didn't know what to say, but I felt like I was close to falling in love with him as well.

Alex called me, asking me why I hadn't come to work for two days, if I was having trouble that he should know about or can help with. I said, "Doug said I was dragged on, I don't need to be dragged on." He laughed, "Ha Ha~ You are not dragged on, report to work tomorrow." Next day, I went to work and Doug came by to say, "I was just kidding, geez, so sensitive, so proud."

I walked into a meeting Steve Thompson was hosting, and everyone turned their head to look, eyes fixed on me quietly. Steve's eyes were frozen on me for a second. I wore my favorite grayish black pant-suite with thin grooves embedded, the sleeves pushed up to just below the elbows, on top of a V-neck casual cotton shell with buttons that had thin stone and black strips across. Every time I wore this set, people stopped to look at me . . . Even the DSIA DIVA Margarette Gundersheimer who always dressed with the most expensive clothes had made comment, "That's a great looking suite! Where did you get that suite?" And I had heard a very sophisticated looking woman at the Chille where I often went for lunch whispering to her friend, "Oh, I love her style!" Even a man, a business man walking passed me on the street commented, "That's the devil!"

When I wanted to look good, I wore this suite. And this time, I wore it to impress Steve Thompson who seemed to try to figure me out. He had invited me to a few meetings (besides the regular project status meetings), and I had spoken very little, still carrying some fear of him asking deep technical stuff at the interview, which I faltered. He seemed almost as technical as Tom. It was fine to be less technical than Tom, but I needed to be more technical than Steve and support him with technical details. I wasn't sure if I would meet his expectation of me. He was a very good manager, no doubt, very clean, yet there was something about him, quietly attractive. Behind his disciplined manners as a manager, he, too, was a man who would appreciate a female, some fun at work that he couldn't have at home, I saw, a wild-streak.

A few engineers sitting nearby my cubicle started to make comments about Tom & me. There was an extremely cynical young guy (a very smart guy) who didn't like Tom hanging around with me (instead of him), and he was trying to pick on me with that awful super jealous Jennifer, who was constantly trying to pick on anything and everything that I did or didn't do. And there was an older contractor woman leading a small task, who seemed grouchy with me being a Karlmon Dietech employee (and her being a contractor). She was complaining to others how I could join Karlmon Dietech through my connection with Alex (vs. my technical qualifications) . . . She shut up after I had clarified the DoD networking that nobody there knew though. However, Jennifer and the cynical short guy kept making an issue out of me and trying to mobilize others against me.

On my way home, I thought about these two. They were not just going to quit attacking me after a while, and I needed to do something about. It was after 6 pm, but I called Mr. Thompson to see if he was still in his office.

"Steve Thompson."
"Hi, this is Chan, ah-, I have some issues that I would like to talk to you about. I am on my way home, and I know it's late. I stopped by your office before I left but you weren't there. Could I come by your office now or should I try to catch you sometime tomorrow?"
"I will be here a little longer."
"It will be about 20 minutes or so for me to drive back."
"Okay, that's fine."

Steve Thompson seemed somewhat surprised but delighted by me requesting a consultation when I walked into his office, saying hi.

"You have some very aggressive employees under you who keep attacking me," I opened the discussion. "I do? Who are they"? He asked, with his eyes lightening up, trying to suppress the smile. I told him what Jennifer was doing to attack me and the various comments that the short guy with smart mouth made about me, about being *yellow* and all. He was aware of Jennifer's behaviors, no doubt, and supported me saying that Jennifer was a secretary for 18 years, had gone through the company career up-mobile program to become a technical associate, and she might be a little jealous of me who were higher than her, with engineering degree. "As for Ken, I am not sure why he is doing that. He is a smart guy. I will talk to him tomorrow and correct the situation," he said.

I had hesitated for weeks trying to decide what to do, putting up with stinky co-workers, and I was glad I consulted with Steve (instead of Alex). Alex was a new manager who brought me into the group, and he could get cornered with a situation like this, I figured. He would need to secure his position as a manager without me troubling him. Most people there had been with the same company for over 15 years, and I had seen how Jennifer was behaving around Alex, closing his office door with her foot when she was entering his office, playing the "power babe." Alex had told mo that Jennifer was good at mobilizing people with her long secretarial experience and advised me to be careful with her.

Steve Thompson had Jennifer order two laptops, one for her and one for me, and when Tom found out, he joked loudly, **"How come you got the brand new laptop? I am the lead engineer, and I am still using the old 486! Ha Ha Ha~"** I said, feeling a little guilty, "Well, that's because I would need to configure the switches and you don't, ne ne ne ne ne~" (I beat you!).

Dan came to my area to have lunch with me (he often did). I asked him to come in to the building and say "hi" to Alex. Alex was delighted by his visit. After chatting with Alex for a few minutes, Dan stuck his face to Steve's office, "How is it going?" Steve looked at Dan and looked at me, surprised. "You two know each other?" Dan smiled and said, "Yes, unfortunately. I knew this lady a long before I met Alex."

Dan and I walked over to a restaurant nearby, which was run by a Korean guy, serving both sandwiches and Chinese buffet. He knew my face as I went there often, smiling with a slight bow, acknowledging me and pleased to see me with Dan, a clean egg-ish guy. We both got the Chinese buffet and sat outside.

"We have an exceptionally good-looking Program Manager. I think he is interested in me." I said, looking at the building across the field where Mr. Goleniewski's office was located.
"You're talking about Tom Goleniewski?" I nodded.
"I know him. He interviewed me, and I thought there is a guy for Chan."
"So how come you didn't tell me about him?"
"I don't know, I just didn't think about him, I guess."
"What do you think about him?"
"I think he will show you good time, but when he is through with you, he will be through with you."

Young Tom was walking by, looking at us, and Dan raised his hand to Tom and Tom raised his hand to Dan. "You know him, too?" I asked, surprised. "Yes, I met him for an interview, too." "Very smart guy" I said. "Yea, he is." Dan said.

Tom took a month off for his annual vacation to Maine, where his parents lived. He said he was going to dip his head in the cool water, taking it easy. No vacation for me this summer.

A week after Tom was gone for vacation with his wife and son, I started to miss him. He was so much fun to be around, always laughing and joking, keeping me entertained . . . I liked everything about him, but it was his personality that swept me off my feet, and maybe vice versa. Maybe he was more taken by my look, but I would guess the look was only the first step.

I liked Steve Thompson, too, and he would probably have appreciated me if I approached him as a guy. So would have Doug. So many guys, one me . . .

OVER MY HEAD CONNECTION

Dave Turgeon, the Business Development Director, at another building across the street, needed an engineer with TCP/IP networking and UNIX knowledge to support him with his new Distance Learning business development activity. Most of the engineers for this group were MBI systems experts, and Alex recommended me for this initiative.

I accompanied Dave for his visit to the TRADOC along with a marketing guy, to help him with technical issues. Dave was the most experienced manager, who retired from MBI as the Business Development Director. He was short, almost shorter than me, 5'4" or so, very generous but tough looking with beard.

Three of us met at a gas station along the Rt. 95 and left our car there. I tried to get into the back seat of Dave's SUV, but the marketing guy asked me to get into the front seat. He was not one of the more talkative marketing guys and probably didn't feel comfortable chatting with Dave, so I would need to entertain Dave during the ride, that meant.

I was prepared. I brought an Astrology book for the trip, and I started to analyze their star signs. Dave became very interested in what astrology said about his Aries personality, as it matched perfectly with himself. He was married to a Scorpio for over 10 years, was unhappy but took a long time to divorce his first wife. Then he married to another Scorpio, and 6 months later, the marriage was over, and he quickly divorced his second wife. He had gone through the divorce experience once, and with no kid, he snapped out his second marriage. Then he stayed single for 10 years and married his third wife, who was working for another Karlmon Dietech Sector. Dave said he'd rather stay away from a Scorpio woman, and I analyzed the problems between Aries guy and Scorpio woman, enthusiastically and laughing a lot since I was a Scorpio myself. Time flew by, and we reached our destination yakking all the way.

The TRADOC Director handed me a document describing their vision for the 21st century distance learning capabilities. I returned with my triumph document and asked Karlmon Dietech engineers to research and investigate the possible solutions for meeting that vision. Tom, of course, was the one who was more than happy to help me with this new venture, joking, "Customers are stealing her from us" . . . When we had some progress, I visited the TRADOC to inform them of our progress and to obtain the further development of their distance learning initiative.

After a few visits, the TRADOC Director provided me with a draft total army distance learning plan for recommendations. He and his staffs, including some military officers, were very acceptable of me, and Dave asked me if I were willing to work at the TRADOC facility for a while. He needed someone to infiltrate the Army training operations. I was new in business development, relatively unprofessional and unwilling to relocate to win the business. I was having fun with Tom, Doug, and a bunch of guys at Karmon Dietech building . . . So I declined.

TRADOC was located in Virginia Beach, about 3 hours driving, and my visit was always just one day trip. But every time I was out visiting the TRADOC, the super jealous Moth made a sarcastic comment, *"Is this that time again?"*

I was late for one of these visits, and Dave had already left the gas station on Rt. 95 where we were supposed to meet. I called him, and we selected another location on Rt. 95, halfway to the TRADOC to link up. When I reached the little rest area, Dave and a new marketing guy were waiting for me, drinking soda. I left my car in the rest area and we drove together as usual.

Dave had arranged a meeting with technical group responsible for implementing and managing the network, and they were asking me about their functional requirements needed to plan their network. How was I supposed to know what their functional requirements were!? Someone from their side should tell us, the potential contractor, what their functional requirements would be!!! Obviously, their functional people and the technical group had not coordinated the requirements for implementing the distance learning capability. I was inexperienced to deal with this kind of situation, and I gave them a short, snappy answer like an unprofessional bimbo implying 'Why the heck are you asking me that!?' Dave quickly covered the uncomfortable situation, suggesting a meeting with both the functional group and the technical group to discuss their requirements.

On our way back home, we stopped at the rest area where I left my car. Dave gave me the instruction on how to turn my car around to head back home, but it sounded confusing. "I don't know if I can do that. Can you turn my car around to where I can walk over?" He tried to figure out what to do for a second, then he told the marketing guy to drive back alone, and he got into my car to drive.

"People are going to think I am a crazy old man driving this pretty pink car." He did look rather goofy sitting at the driver seat of my sexy metallic pink Probe. "Ha ha~ you look just fine. Besides, you are the first guy driving my car," I flattered him. "Oh, so I should feel honored?" he laughed. That was exactly what I liked about him, very comfortable, even though he was much older.

We drove back to the gas station on Rt. 95, and he asked me, "Do you want to have some beer?" I didn't mind having some beer after the stress I was under in the frustrating meeting, but I was reluctant to start any kind of wrong personal relationship with him, "Maybe next time. I am very tired today." He looked disappointed for a split of second, but he was cool, "OK, go home and get some rest. See you later, kiddo!" He always called me kiddo, and I liked him calling me kiddo, like he was my uncle, someone who would be very generous to me and fond of me despite my shortcomings.

Dave had me officially transferred to his Business Development Group, moving me to the building-1 where he was. I continued to visit the TRADOC and evaluated the COTS systems and applications suitable for the distance learning capabilities that the Army needed, building ongoing working relationship with the Army training people.

BEST HUMAN RESOURCES

Building-1 was for Business Development, Marketing, Administration people and associated contractors. The first thing I noticed was that there were a lot more women in this building. A bunch of older women hung around together, running their mouths, gossiping about everything.

Tom Goleniewski was at this building, and I could see him every morning through his office window when walking toward the building from the parking lot. He looked like Da BOSS, sitting on his high-back chair, just looking magnificent! He was in his 50's, just perfect looking from top to bottom. He looked like he defined the word, the BOSS, or some gorgeous modern King of Denmark, making me think of the Lion King. He was a great leader, with people waiting in front of his office in lines, generating Goleniewski Flow. Whatever he did, it soared!

He had seen me a few times in different meetings, and when I first learned that he might be interested in me, I was more than thrilled. I felt like a winner, more than I deserved, and I couldn't help smiling, smiling by myself trying not to be noticed by anyone of my inner-satisfied smile. Wow, a guy like him liking me?

It was when I was working on the CUITN project that everyone thought he might be interested in me, and young Tom was getting nervous. And I was having trouble deciding who I would like more? "We don't talk about dropping something here," Doug had made his sharp sarcastic remark, making me feel guilty.

I wanted to let Tom Goleniewski know that I was thrilled by him, but what could I do? A few weeks after I had moved to Building-1, I sent him an e-mail from my AOL e-mail account that I specifically had made for him, telling him that I needed to test my AOL e-mail connectivity and I had to test it with him because my e-mail address contained part of his last name. He must have laughed hard at my stupid but cute move that his secretary Kate gave me a very unusual look (surprised, jealous, nervous, concerned, . .).

Tom broadcasted e-mails to everyone regarding the program status and other company-related information, and people interpreted them like he was sending some hidden messages to me . . I was hoping for that myself anyway, and I was going crazy, trying to catch the hidden messages, wondering whether I was supposed to do something or not.

People came to talk about Tom's e-mails with an old woman contractor who sat next to me, Linda, opcculating something between the lines, driving me crazy. Dave Turgeon was avoiding me and he had not come in to the office for a few days, and with that, I mustered enough courage to call Mr. Goleniewski and asked him to meet me at the Chille during the lunch time. I couldn't make myself walk into his office with all the vague, speculating noises.

Tome came but he looked very uncomfortable, so uncomfortable that his face hardened for a second when I looked at him (he couldn't even look at me). He glimpsed at my whisky-sour sitting on the table and ordered a coke. I talked him about Dave Turgeon, how he seemed to have some concerns about me and people coming to Linda to gossip . . I had my cell-phone on the table (my cheap cell-phone was too bulky to fit in my handbag), and he took out his sleek cell-phone from his jacket pocket and put it on the table. Okiedokie!

I asked Dave to bring young Tom to his group, but Dave said he would need a heavy hitter like Tom later, not right away. Young Tom left Karlmon Dietech and went to work for a new venture company as Technical Director.

People kept gossiping about Mr. Goleniewski & me, Dave & me, and then Dave was going to fire me. 'Fire me for what reason?' I thought, and a few days later, Alex, my old boss, told me that the HR Director from the Owego HQ would be at our facility, talking to some of the employees, and I would be one of them. "Why me?" I asked Alex, and he said it was just random selections.

The HR Director was another exceptionally good looking guy. Not so much over-the-top looking as Tom, but he looked good enough to be a movie star as well, more reserved and sincere looking. He introduced himself to me and mumbled, "small site." Apparently, I was less than what he had expected. First Tom, and now this HR Director, they were so darn gorgeous, being on top of the world, 'Who would be good enough for them?' I wondered. I had never thought of myself as exceptionally good-looking, actually surprised that there weren't any better looking females in the organization.

The HR Director asked me how I transferred to Dave's group and how my work was going . . . "Dave brought me into his group to make me his trip companion, I believe. He is a womanizer." The HR Director seemed a bit surprised by my bold remark and said, "Womanizer is a strong word." So I went on telling him about Dave's behaviors toward me. "Dave had called me into his office, and when I entered his office, he had his feet on the desk with legs wide open. I was surprised and had to look away while I was talking to him. He was even sliding down on his chair, almost getting laid down on his chair. I believe Dave is aggressive, outgoing and straightforward, but what he did to me seemed like a sexual harassment." The HR Director John Krause, gave me his business card and said, "Please call me if you need my help."

Right after my meeting with Mr. John Krause was over, Tom Goleniewski broadcasted an e-mail stating, "WINNER, one of the few I met who is very comfortable being oneself." Alex gave me the thumb up with a big smile when I ran into him, so I must have impressed the HR Director.

After that, I called John when I got frustrated with people attacking me, with my cell-phone, at the parking lot, to avoid people overhearing (or listening to) my conversations with him. I let my frustration out on him complaining to him about what some "stupid little people" were doing to me. Unlike Tom, John was reliable who communicated with me directly, and with him on my side (or knowing that I was communicating with him), people treated me well. He was the most mature and fair human-being with good heart and lazer-sharp eyes, who became my human role model.

PERFECT COMPANY PARTY

Karlmon Dietech got additional funding to continue the Army program, and Mr. Goleniewski invited everyone working on his Army programs for a Potomac River Cruise, all company-paid. His secretary Kate brought me an elegant ivory invitation card with letters written in gold. It kept me excited, thinking about seeing and spending time with Tom on this cruise party.

Most people came with their spouses, but I went by myself. It was a chilly November night, and I wore a blue mustang coat that my sister bought me, with ivory sweater and brown pants to match the brown fir on the coat. I rarely wore this coat because it looked too rich and seemed to annoy people, but it was a special occasion, so why not? I spotted Dave standing in the line with his wife, who was with another Karlmon Dietech Sector, and he was looking at me up and down, smiling big (drooling).

Everyone was dressed up for the party, and I felt like I was under-dressed except the coat, wearing sweater and pants, instead of some shiny silk dress or something more formal like most other women were wearing, but too late.

My table was near the entrance. It was the table for the singles who didn't bring anyone along, the loser table. I had a friend who I'd been hanging around with, a typical Irish looking single guy with a lot of freckles and red hair, at the same table, so I was pretty comfortable.

Tom came alone, sitting with high-level managers. Kate walked over to my table and stood behind one of the better-looking females, Jessica, with her hands on the back of Jessica's chair, looking at Tom's table. Apparently, she was trying to draw Tom's eyes to Jessica. I had seen Jessica in the restroom sometimes, but I didn't know what she was doing, had never talked to her, other than saying "hi." She looked like a cold stuck-up bitch with nagging personality and no-brainer looking with thick eye makeup. No winner to my eyes.

After the dinner, I walked around the deck with my good-heart friend, feeling the chilling wind of the river. I looked inside to see what Tom was doing, and I caught his eyes and turned my head quickly around. The bend played music for dancing, and I was one of the first few knuckleheads who got up to dance, being the carefree single and as a younger member. I was dancing away for every song, spinning and sweating . . .

Tom was wearing a black polar sweater and black pants under grey jacket, looking darn sexy and gorgeous. He was just walking around to make sure that everything was well, and someone hinted me to dance with him. I drank a few more whisky-sours fast. Tom was talking with some guy, another manager, and I walked over to them and said to the manager, "Would you mind talking to him later" with a demanding tone. He smiled and said, "Oh, sorry" and walked away fast.

Tom looked uncomfortable, standing there with me alone, looking at the manager who was walking away, like he wanted to say "Please stay with me." I put both of my hands on Tom's arm and try to drag him to the dance floor. He said, "Oh, no, I don't want to . . " I dragged his arm a little harder, and he came along. I put my arm on his shoulder, and he placed his hand on my back, holding my hand with the other hand, lightly and very smoothly. I felt like the whole world was mine at that moment, feeling indescribably floating, happy and thrilled . . . .

Everyone was watching us, and my old boss, Alex, smiled at me with surprised eyes. The last few quick drinks must have circulated my body, as I was getting very bold, not thinking clearly. I wanted to put my other arm around his neck, but he wouldn't let me, holding my hand tight. I tried one more time, and he held my hand tighter, restraining me. 'Okay, I'd better behave myself. It is not a good idea in front of everyone who works for him,' I was behaving badly.

He was big and I felt so good being so close to him, I put my body closer to his body and leaned my head on his chest. It felt very comfortable and felt dizzy at the same time.

It was the most exciting and thrilling moment of my professional life . .

EXECUTIVES' GOLF TOURNAMENT

Tom got promoted as Senior Vice President and had to move to the Owego HQ in New York State. He sent out an e-mail, implying that each and everyone was important to him, nobody was special. Some guy walked by my cubicle, saying, "That was a bomb!" He needed to clear himself of me, to move away, that meant, I thought. Or he needed to clear the illusion that his e-mails had generated . .

Dave came by my cubicle, all jolly, and said, "Let's go out and have a cigarette." I didn't feel like smoking cigarette with him at that moment and told him that I didn't have any cigarette. "I give you mine," he said. Okay, he was my boss, and he must have some burning desire to talk to me. We walked through the back door to get to the company backyard, and there were some people smoking and chatting . . . Dave gave me one of his cigarettes and lighted it up for me, which he often did.

"Have you been to Owego?"

"No, I haven't."

"Would you consider moving up there?"

"If I move up there, I will be working from 7 o'clock in the morning to 9 o'clock at night."

"Why? Oh, because nothing to do up there? Ha ha~"

"What did you do when you were working up there? I understand it's a pretty remote area?"

"Yea, there isn't much around to do for recreation, really. I worked there for 7 years, just working, well, I did some fishing."

"It's like a redneck area, isn't it? My ex-husband's family had a small place in Pennsylvania mountain area, near Scranton. And we went to a local bar once, and the moment I walked into the door, everybody stared at me, like I was an ET or something. I was very uncomfortable, and my ex-husband asked me if I wanted to leave, but I decided to have a couple of drinks. We sat at a bar, and some guys came around and stood right next to me and stared at me, trying to make me uncomfortable, trying to make me leave. Then somebody dropped something heavy, making a scary noise. We left after one drink. I could just imagine what would happen if I went into a bar by myself. I imagine Owego may be similar?"

"Probably close. I didn't like up there. I am building a place in the lake where I will retire to."

"What lake? Is it in this area?"

"Yea, it's in Maryland."

"Do you have a boat?"

"Yea, I do."

People were looking at Dave and me, and some guy gave me a cold look when he was going inside, like he was thinking 'Don't you have any feeling for Tom Goleniewski going away?' What was I supposed to do? I was sad, but I didn't want people to know how I was feeling.

The Army Program Infrastructure Manager, Tony, got promoted as the new Program Manager, and not long after Tom moved to Owego, Kate sent out an e-mail containing the word M&M, then passed out the *M&M*

chocolates to everyone in the building. People came to talk to Linda, the old loud mouth contractor woman, implying that I was to be Tony's and Dave's babe now, driving me crazy. She loved bitching about me, of course (the closer, the more jealous, and in this case, it was sitting next to me), and for this, she almost shouted, "**Oh, My God! They are going to sandwich her!**" Some women were more open-minded about, saying, "Why not? I'll do it." And some said I would have to leave the building if I rejected this sandwich thing . .

I ignored people's comments and just tried to focus on my work. Knowing that I had no intention of playing this sandwich thing, Linda was trying to rally people against me, making an announcement proudly, "I am old, so if I get kicked out for doing this, that's okay." She had been working too long, maybe. I had introduced myself to her when I first moved to this building, and I sensed that she was going to be negative toward me, no matter what I did (or didn't do), looking at me with totally resisting eyes. She did say, "the best one yet, feisty and all." She started display-ing ridiculous things on top of her cubicle wall, such as an empty milk carton or some strange-looking stuffed animals as a means to attack me.

Another e mail was sent out by Kate with the word "chicken breast breast" informing everyone of the company picnic. It was one of the menu items, and I just replied to Kate that I would have the chicken breast. People were going around making comments about this e-mail as well. Men were compassionate, saying to Linda, "Geez, I don't want to be under the pressure like that" or "That's gotta be tough shoes to be in." Linda shouted "**Yellow**" in the hallway, and I just ignored her considering her behavior as the old-age hysterical outburst coming from living with her 90-some year old Mom.

The picnic was held at the yard behind the building on Friday, and I went to work wearing T-shirt and blue jeans for the picnic. Dave was wearing a suite, as usual, and he whispered to me, "I feel like a dork wearing a suite." I laughed and said, "You can take off the jacket and pull up the shirt sleeves."

There was a dunk game setup. Alex, my old boss, was sitting at the dunk chair, and people lined up to throw a ball at him! They were all missing, and Alex was still sitting there looking a little awkward. I watched for a while and got in the line. A young contractor guy who was passing the ball to everyone gave me a worried look, reluctant to give me a ball. I took my right hand out and said, "Give me the ball!" holding a piece of cookie I was eating in my left hand.

I had watched baseball often enough and imitated the pitcher's form and pitched at Alex, and BOOM! He fell into the water! I was the first one who succeeded, and I felt darn good, extremely proud of myself. People were wow'ing, clapping, laughing and smiling. Some guys got challenged and tried to throw the ball again, but all failed. The next one who was able to dunk Alex was Doug, the cool TA&T single guy. "Whew", he said, smiling. I gave him V-sign, smiling.

After Alex had been dunked twice, Tony was on the dunk chair, but I decided not to try to dunk him. Ms. Moth was trying to dunk him, and after failing three times, she walked to the dunk board and pushed it with her hand to dunk Tony. She was after him. I had seen her putting one leg on a chair with legs open position at one of the all-hands meeting hosted by him. I thought that was pretty darn unattractive.

I ran into Alex going inside of the building, his suites all wet and dripping, and he gave me a big smile, saying, "You got a great arm!" I raised my right arm to show him my *muscled* arm.

Finally, I had chance to visit the Owego facility, to attend a networking conference hosted by a PhD guy, an Iranian, who was managing the network research lab. It was much larger than the Springfield facility, with manufacturing facility included. I ran into John looking for the conference room, and he was surprised to see me, asking, "What are you doing here?"

After the conference, I had a meeting with this PhD guy, to discuss the Army distance learning networking possibilities, and darn, he was touching my leg with his foot. I wanted to say, "Stop that stupid thing!" but I just gave him a cold look, and he stopped.

My new boss welcomed me, providing me with temporary work space and introducing me to other engineers working for him. I spent three days to check the networking capabilities and activities going on at the Owego facility. During my visit, I went to see Tom to say "hi," but he wasn't at his office. I stopped by his office one more time, before I left the building, but he was in a meeting again. I left a new DoD standard document to his secretary and left the building.

Next day, Tom sent down a bunch of e-mails about successfully *installing some system* and other activities, and his e-mails infuriated Linda. She almost screamed hysterically, "That's disgusting!" Geez, I didn't even get to see his gorgeous face that women at the Owego facility were drooling over, as I heard.

Tom came down every once in a while hosting all-hands meeting. One of the all-hands meetings occurred on my birthday, and I asked Jerry to buy me my birthday-lunch. Jerry said he would take me out to lunch if Tom didn't (I knew Tom wouldn't take me out to lunch for my birthday). I briefly saw Tom after the meeting, and he looked like he wanted to turn around to look at me turning his head about 10 degree, paused for about 1 second, and left without saying anything. What's that!?

People kept making noises about me every time the Program Manager's office sent out e-mails, and I forwarded some e-mails broadcasted by Tony's office to Tom. My boss and John, the HR Director, came down from Owego, and we met at an office that had been vacant ever since I moved to the Building-1. It was a relatively large office with 4 red guest chairs making it look pretty, and some people had speculated that I might be moving into this office.

My boss said, "Chan, I told you not to contact Mr. Goleniewski. He is very busy, and he doesn't read your e-mails. His secretary reads all of his e-mails." Geez, I could just imagine how Owego people would have been gossiping about Tom & me. I must have put him into an uncomfortable situation. "People are making comments about him and me here all the time and I thought he should know about," I said. "What kinds of comments? Are you talking about the fountain talk?" My boss asked. My new boss was a retired Marine Colonel, who was very sincere and straightforward. "Yes, people come by Linda Horvatt's cubicle all the time, making all kinds of comments about the e-mails Mr. Goleniewski sends down in conjunction with me."

"E-mails? What kind of e-mails does he send down?" The HR Director asked. "Oh, he sends down e-mails all the time, describing the functions of the organization, new projects, some company policies, program status and things like that." I answered. "I see. That's normal practice, so why would people relate those e-mails to you and make comments about?" He asked, looking puzzled. "I don't know why, but apparently, they think he is trying to tell me something with those e-mails," I answered. "That may be just your perception," John said, and I snapped, "If you go out and ask any of these people, they will tell you that there is something going on between Tom and me."

My boss jumped in, "Chan, if you have any concerns with people's comment about you, you tell me or tell Mr. Krause. Or ask David Turgeon to help you resolve the situation since he is around and will know what's going on better. I cannot emphasize enough that you should not contact Mr. Goleniewski for anything. Do you understand the seriousness?" I sighed and said, "Dave is one of the people making those comments!" Both my boss and John looked surprised, looking at each other.

"Mr. Dave Turgeon makes comments about Mr. Goleniewski and you?" My boss asked, "What sort of comments does he make?" I'd rather not drag Dave down for this, but I had no choice but to let them know of the situation to defend myself. "Yes, he visits Linda Horvatt to make all kinds of comments about those e-mails, and as a matter of fact, when I came back from visiting the Owego facility, he even said to me, "Are you all fucked up now?"" They looked at each other again (going What!?). "When did Dave say that to you?" John asked. "The day I came back, around 1 o'clock or so, when I ran into him at the hallway, near the copy machine there" I answered, pointing to where the copy machine was located through the door. John looked down and said to himself, "I am going to have to talk to Dave."

"There is something I need to tell you," I said to my boss, "I am diagnosed with the breast cancer so I need to take some time off." My boss' eyes widened, totally surprised, and his face softened from feeling sorry for me, "When did you learn that?" "Yesterday," I said calmly, "I had a small lump and had it removed and got the biopsy done, and the doctor says it's a cancer." I tried hard to hold off tears, but I just couldn't, tears were forming in my eyes. "We have good medical plan and doctors who can help you," John said. "Thank you, my ex-husband is in the medical field and he is helping me," I said and tears were just dropping down on my cheek. "Do you need some tissue?" John asked, and I nodded. He went out and brought me a box of tissue and left quickly.

For the moment, I didn't care where I was, I just felt sorry for myself being so unlucky, felt like my life was over and couldn't stop crying. My boss was just sitting there watching me compassionately, and he said, "My wife had the breast cancer a few years ago and her Mom also had the breast cancer. So I know what you are going through. Let me know if there is anything I can do to help." I couldn't say anything. He sat there watching me cry for a while, then he left.

I sat in the empty office a little longer, trying to get a hold of myself and waiting for my eyes to look normal, not red or swollen. Then I came out, hoping that nobody would notice that I had cried. I didn't know how long I stayed in that office. When I came out, it was dark outside, and most people had left.

John must have called Tom about my situation while I was sitting in that office crying my eyeballs out. There was an e-mail about breast cancer and another e-mail about the project my red hair friend was working on. That was his way of asking my friend to help me get through the breast cancer, apparently.

Illusion was what I was dealing with, as John pointed out, not just one's illusion but everyone's illusion. Someone said 'history was the illusion of historians, dealing with facts. Everyone was reading between the lines, generating the illusion of illusion, depending on each one's state of mind.

I interpreted broadcasted e-mails as I wished, towards the direction of making me feel good, more or less, possibly, and those who didn't like me probably interpreted as they wished, towards the direction of attacking me, possibly far away from sender's intention sometimes. It could have just been the secretary who sent out some of these broadcasted e-mails, on her own, to inform others or to generate the atmosphere she wanted, playing THE boss.

When I returned to the office after going through the surgery and radiology treatment, Tom broadcasted an e-mail welcoming my return with *embracing* something message. People came by my office to ask me how I was feeling . . . I felt fine. I just had a tiny lump close to my arm-fit and it was no big deal after the initial dismay. "You look damn good!" someone said, smiling . . .

Two days after I returned to the office, Dave scheduled a briefing for me at Tony's office for Distance Learning project status. Apparently Dave's intention for me was negative (My gut feeling was that he was looking for a reason to fire me off). He hadn't shown any compassion for my illness, looking uncomfortable and saying, "That sounds scary" when I told him about the radiology treatment. My boss was trying to postpone the briefing to give me some time, a week or so at least, for me to get back on track and catch up with my task. I told my boss that I could handle the briefing just fine.

Dave attended the briefing from the Owego facility, and he was trying to pick on me with every details, but I was well-prepared as I had been communicating with one of the guys supporting Dave during my absence, answering every question clearly. *Eye-to-eye, nose-to-nose*, head-to-head, I questioned him for unclear directions. His voice got lowered. So low that people could barely hear what he was saying and I had to ask him to speak a little louder. My boss smiled at me when the briefing was over, telling me that I did very well. (I patted myself on the back for being so cool.)

Tom came to the Distance Learning Trade Show held in Colorado. I tried to carry on a small conversation with him when he came by our booth, but he never seemed to be comfortable talking with me, always saying very little. For this trade show, I was working as a technical lead and as an exhibitor as well since the new marketing guy wasn't knowledgeable enough with the systems I set up for the exhibits. I used my hands and cute gestures to entertain the customers visiting our booth, and the marketing manager was very pleased with how I was managing my extra task, thanking me and asking me to help his new guy get started . . .

During the break, I walked around the exhibition hall to check other vendors. I went out to get something to drink and spotted Tom standing alone, drinking something, looking uptight and lonely. I thought about walking over to him and chat with him for a few minutes, but I didn't think he would appreciate my company at that moment. He looked just very alone.

There was a dinner party scheduled on the first night and I was hoping Tom would join this dinner party, but he didn't come, just the marketing guys and Jan, the tradeshow coordinator from the Owego facility. After a few drinks, I danced with the marketing guys and dragged the Marketing Manager to the dance floor. He and I danced like maniacs, turning and spinning, and sweating. When we returned to our seat, guys laughed at their boss, and Jan gave me a surprised, dirty look! She was a nice very mom-like upper-class woman, and apparently she didn't expect me to be so bold and carefree with the Marketing Manager who was much older than me, who was more in her league.

When the trade show was over and everyone had left, I, the only engineer in the team, needed to pack the equipment and ship them back. Paul, the senior marketing guy, helped me packing, and he joked, "This is a high-level Karlmon Dietech engineering job!"

I had a big Black guy supporting me with packing and shipping at the office, a subcontractor, and he had asked me, "How could I get to do what you are doing?" "Well, I started with a degree in Electrical Engineering, and I have several years of experience working as a network engineer. If you are interested in doing what I am doing, I would suggest you start taking classes."

Tony's office kept sending out e-mails, and people kept making comments about these e-mails in conjunction with me . . I briefed him on the distance learning business development status once a month, as he requested. I saw him tucking his shirts when he saw me, but other than that, he hadn't tried to pressure me or anything. Nevertheless, I was getting pressured by people's comments and worried that I could be causing undesirable tension between the Executives. The Facility Manager was posting the messages in different colors on everyone's door and making announcements implying my status with a loudspeaker. Even the Helpdesk subcontractors were shooting e-mails constantly.

I was getting stressed out from these e-mails and people's comments, and I forwarded some of the e-mails to my boss and the HR Director with people's comments. Next day, my boss came down from Owego and told me that I needed to take some time off . . . .

I had a lot of respect for both my boss and the HR Director. They were the good kind who became compassionate in my bad situation, never overpowering or arrogant, disciplined but fair and compassionate. That would be the most matured form of mankind, I would imagine, and I felt lucky to have them around . . .

BUSINESS DEVELOPMENT & MARKING ENGINEER

I had taken 4 months time-off, and as I walked into the building, the Facility Manager played the "welcome" music, "**BB~aam bbara bbaam bbaa bbaa~~~~**"

They must have been bored while I was gone. I used the backdoor to enter the building, trying not to get noticed, but they must have seen my pink car pulling into the parking lot. I was the only one driving that yucky color car as Jennifer had referred as (almost pissed off at my car color) when she first saw it.

There was a new guy, Jerry, and some other new faces, under Dave's Group. Jerry was a clean and playful looking guy, in his 50's, and he stated "1069!" when he first met me at a meeting. Later, he introduced himself to me as a "wild hunting dog." When I visited his office, he joked, "My next wife will be an Asian." I didn't say anything. He probably didn't know what was going on there, I thought. In any case, he found out soon enough, as people started shooting e-mails again . . . .

I worked closely with Paul, who was the senior marketing guy for the distance learning program. He was a very cool Italian guy, who used to be an engineer (with electrical engineering degree). Jerry, Paul, and I became a team for the distance learning business opportunities, visiting and briefing potential customers. Jerry coordinated various meetings, and Paul started referring him as a "Meeting man." Both Jerry and Paul were super talkers, and when three of us visited potential customers, I didn't need to say much. I just needed answer a few technical questions.

The part of the Building-1 had been remodeled, and Dave had me move into one of the new offices. A few days later, the Facility Manager had a fat Black contractor-woman doing the administration work move into the office right next to my office. I thought Paul deserved an office more than me (and a lot more than a dumb-looking contractor), but he never said anything about it. He was too cool to make an issue out of such a thing.

I asked Paul to a meeting with a video conferencing system vendor that I had arranged to discuss the possibility of integrating a video conferencing system into our distance learning solution packages. He talked almost for two hours, non-stop, with the marketing representative of the video conferencing systems. No chance for a slow talker like myself to jump in, going "ah-, eh-."

Sometimes, I sat on the bench across the parking lot behind the building, taking a little break, smoking cigarette or reading some document. Other smokers just looked at me from the smoking area, just behind the back-door, but Dave would walk over to me, sitting on the bench with me, asking, "What's up, kiddo?" He and I had some kind of 'love and hate' relationship. He was the one who I felt most comfortable with, but at the same time, he seemed to want to get rid of me.

I asked Dave for a raise, and he really got pissed off at me! People assumed that I had moved up with a higher salary and had higher expectation of me. 'I am reporting to the Business Development Director, not a regular low-level manger here, and I am doing higher-level work in his group,' I had justified myself. I thought I might be being a chicken not asking for a salary raise I should have. Dave looked at me like I was being ridiculous and told me to focus on doing good work for three years, and he might think about raising my salary. I could tell from the look on his face that if I ever mentioned it again, he would kick me out!

Jerry and Dave were alike in some ways, extremely energetic and almost hyper-active. The Building-1 was well air-conditioned, but these two needed extra cooling. Jerry had a small desktop fan but Dave had a huge floor fan, always on, while there were some people needing sweaters. It must be the business development guy thing, I could only conclude. They made me wonder how much more body heat they generated . . . ?

For the Navy distance learning program, I worked with Karlmon Dietech Government Systems (KDGS) located in New Jersey, preparing a joint-proposal. This group's lead engineer was a retired Air force guy, Chuck, and he invited me to come up to their facility to learn the capabilities of the information management system that they had developed. Jerry and Paul accompanied me for this visit. It was a relatively small off-site building, and when we entered the building, the Director came out to greet us. Jerry introduced himself, Paul, and me, proudly stating, "Chan is an Electrical Engineer!" The KDGS Director was pleased, "That's great! Hi Chan!" and took us to a meeting room where several guys were sitting and chatting, all White guys.

After the meeting, Jerry and Paul stayed in the room to chat with guys there, and Chuck took me to the lab to demonstrate their information management system. It was a very complicated system, and it took all afternoon to see the demo and obtain enough information on this system. Jerry had arranged a meeting with another group there, and he and Paul briefed them of our group's distance learning program and capabilities.

It was a long day, starting at 7am, driving for two hours, and by the time we left the building, I was exhausted. Jerry and Paul kept non-stop conversation for two more hours driving back home. Some engineer guy had told me that marketing guys were different animal when I was transferring to the business development group. Engineers don't talk much, and these two never got tired of running their mouths. Dan had told me once that I would have made an excellent marketing person, but I had a long way to catch up on these guys.

There was a briefing and demonstration scheduled for an Army General. I coordinated the demo with our distance learning partner companies, integrating video conferencing system, teaching tools and courseware development systems. My teammate, Pat, came down from Owego and a young CEO who developed a courseware development system flew down from Boston. Other participants were local.

I was in charge of a bunch of top-notch guys (our partners), feeling good, despite the young CEO commenting me as a "power point" in an attempt to put me down. Kate provided lunch for everyone for two days, carrying the sandwich trays to the conference room where I was setting up the demo system. Yes, I'd much rather be an engineer than a secretary, just for that.

Tom came down from Owego, and I was wondering whether I should attend this meeting or not. They would need an engineer to answer the technical questions, but Dave didn't tell me to attend the meeting. He had Doug, the TA&T guy, attend the meeting instead of me..

Doug used to joke how he had to do the boring job of setting up the systems for the distance learning tradeshows and I get to do the fun job of going to the tradeshows, but for this occasion, it was the other way around. He was a contractor but he was a more experienced engineer, and apparently Dave had more confidence in him. Doug was making a lot more money than I was, no doubt.

After the briefing to the General, the marketing manager came by to thank me for setting up the system beautifully. Then Paul came by to thank me for doing a great job, with a guilty look, telling me that everything went very well and the General was very pleased with the system. He needed someone to disconnect the system and move the equipment out of the conference room. I was the low life who needed to clean up the party that I didn't attend. As I was unhooking the wires feeling sorry for myself, Jerry peeked in and asked me if I needed some help. I said, "Sure, I need someone to move these two PC's to the lab, but you don't have to do, I can ask Rich to do that." It didn't look right for a well-dressed business development guy to carry PCs around, but Jerry seemed happy to do. He made me feel better.

Tom came down to get the status of Navy distance learning program. Dave was attending the briefing from Owego, and two Navy Program Managers briefed Tom. I was there to clarify the technical issues. Tom asked about the Information Management System (IMS) developed by the

Karlmon Dietech Government Systems, "Can we use the KDGS IMS for the Navy proposal?" He made me super nervous and tickled at the same time, and I answered looking into his eyes, wondering about our little Internet plays, "It's an over-kill." I couldn't say any more than that. He looked at me, and asked, "It's an over-kill?" And all I could say was, "Yes." He quickly turned his eyes away from me and continued to ask other non-technical questions to the Program Managers. I was just thrilled to be sitting next to him, hoping he wouldn't ask any questions that I would need to answer.

I coordinated a meeting with Karlmon Dietech Government Systems in New Jersey and Karlmon Dietech Mission Systems in Florida for a Navy distance learning proposal that we were working on as the joint effort. I arranged the Conference Room 6, putting the tables in U-shape with the projector at the front. Dave had not been in the office for a week, and I asked Kate to inform him of this meeting.

When my guests arrived at 11:00 o'clock, Kate brought in a large sandwich tray and a vegetable tray. She looked a little embarrassed carrying the trays in when I looked at her. I had just asked her to contact Dave for this meeting since he wasn't around for a few days, but she did a wonderful job! Everyone was pleased, and Kathy, the Program Manager from Karlmon Dietech Mission Systems, who was the only other woman besides myself, said, "Wow, it looks great. Thanks Chan, for doing this."

Kathy was much more experienced than me in the industry, with a PhD degree. However, I was in the center of this proposal because of my networking expertise, and also because I was with Karlmon Dietech

Systems Integration Sector supporting Dave Turgeon, Business Development Director.

I wrote the Introduction and Networking sections by myself, and Cost and Contract sections with Dave's help, and I integrated the Systems and Applications sections written by Kathy's group and Chuck's group. Each group prepared briefing charts for the distance learning systems used by their group, and I coordinated the working sessions to modify and integrate the briefing charts.

Kathy was selected as the briefer to the Navy representatives. Dave couldn't come to the briefing, and I asked Doug to attend the briefing but he declined. Doug had provided some input for the proposal, but he probably didn't feel comfortable. Besides Kathy, I was the only Karlmon Dietech representative sitting on the front seat to answer questions.

We won some piece of the Navy distance learning project.

CHRISTMAS BABE . .

I kept thinking that I needed to leave the Company to get away from Tom. He was no help to me, and I was no help to him, turning people away with our virtual little relationship. Dave Turgeon must have sensed that I might be planning to leave when I asked him for some time off and told me not to take off, just leaving some vacation request paperwork somewhere (like an unprofessional knucklehead). I laughed and asked him for two months off to go see my family in Korea.

When I returned to work, I found that Dave had changed the owner of the Distance Learning Lab. The lab was my idea, and I had coordinated all of the equipment there, working with the Facility Manager to get me the lab space and working with the vendors for the test equipment/system. Just my name was posted on the lab door before my vacation, and it was changed to Dave Turgeon, Jack Kineriem, Robert Hale, and me as a backup while I was gone. The loud mouth old woman Linda was laughing at me when I was looking at the lab door, dumbfound, thinking '*what is this!?*'

I suggested Jack to join Karlmon Dietech when his company was closing down. He was a former Karlmon Dietech employee and was working as director for one of our distance learning partner companies, a small and relatively new company. Jack was a young single guy, very professional and clean, who everyone liked, and Dave brought him into Karlmon Dietech within a week as a project manager. Bob was a new engineer for my group who transferred from another Karlmon Dietech group, an old guy in his late 60's, totally cynical. "I gotta be the baby-sitter here, hah!" he mumbled soon after he joined my group, like someone asked him to be. I certainly didn't ask him to do anything other than the technical work that he was hired to do. Everything was "Hah!" to him.

I complained this lab steal to Tom at night on the Internet since I was not allowed to contact him. He couldn't care less, just telling me not to be concerned. As far as he was concerned, I didn't need to work hard or try to be important with big responsibility. Even if he didn't like what others were doing to me, what could he do, kick their ass for stealing my lab? He would just get cornered, if he did.

One evening, Doug came by office. "Hi there," he said, sitting down on the floor of my office door leaning against the door post. Dave had funded Doug to work as a consultant for the distance learning program, and I'd been working with him on and off. He was the only other engineer from my old Engineering Group who Dave had picked up for his Business Development activities.

"Hi, what's up?"
"Oh, nothing much, just felt like chatting with you. How was your vacation to Korea?"
"It was pretty good. I don't get to see my family often, and I took a little trip to Thailand and Hong Kong with my Mom and my sister."
"Sounds like you've had a great vacation. Your Mom must have been very happy."

"Yea, she was. She lives with my brother and his family, and she needed a break, badly."

"I am getting back with my ex-wife, tired of being single."

"Are you? Why did you leave your marriage in the first place?"

"Well, I thought I might find someone better, but they are all the same."

"Hope it works out better this time."

"Yea, I hope so, too. It's my son really. I want to have my son around."

"Sure, compromise is what is needed for successful marriage, someone told me."

"I am not going to compromise more than I have. I love my son, and I want to provide him with a good home."

"That's good. I don't have kid, so I don't know, but they say kids keep you going . . . By the way, I have a question for you."

"Okay, shoot."

"I brought an electronic device from Korea that takes 220 volts, and I need a converter. Where can I get the 220 to 110 volt converter?"

"What is it?"

Oops! I didn't think about him asking me that question. I blushed.

"I am not going to tell you what it is."

"Why not? HA HA~"

"It's a female thing."

"Ha ha~ There is Steve's Electronics on the Columbia Pike, right off 495, they may have the converter you need. Or even Radio Shack may have some converters."

"Oh, okay, I can check that store this weekend, I guess."

I saw him when he was leaving the office, and he looked like an old English gentleman, wearing the tan trench coat and a hat. Somehow, his outfit didn't seem to match his personality. I always thought he was a very casual guy, more as a guy who would wear a leather bomber jacket, and even thought about dating him (with the possibility of marriage). Thought he would make a nice responsible and protective, handy-man husband. His outfit made him look like a stranger, all of a sudden.

Kate was eliminating me in some meeting invitations that she was sending out on behalf of Dave Turgeon, and Dave must have caught what she was doing. She came to my office concerning a Dave's meeting and apologized, "It won't happen again." Then I noticed a department meeting invitation that she (accidentally) eliminated my stronger supporter, Paul. I told Paul about the meeting, and he looked uneasy. I was aware that Kate had been passing out something to people, trying to rally people against me.

My team mate, Bob, was passing me e-mails that he received from Doug, apparently to tell me that Doug was eliminating me for his network engineering discussion which was my expertise as well as his. Bob was also back-copying me on the e-mails that he was sending to others. I was annoyed by him doing that, but I didn't say anything, suspecting his intention for doing that was cheap. He was one of those sneaky kinds and too old for still doing the device configuration, looking like a grandpa.

Bob and I went to San Francisco for a training of the video conferencing system that we were planning to use, which lasted for five days. One of my old high-school friends from Korea, a PhD, was visiting California for a week to study Silicon Valley's technology development on the same week. She was staying at a hotel in San Jose run by a Korean-American, and I drove an hour to pick her up at her hotel every evening to have dinner with her. That was good. I didn't feel like having dinners with this Bob guy, really.

Tom Goleniewski reorganized the group, and Dave was named as the head of new Telecommunications business development (instead of Distance Learning) with nobody under him yet. I thought I should be in his group since I was the telecommunications expert, but I was still in the Distance Learning group with a new boss located in Owego. My team members were wondering whether I would be transferred to Dave's group soon after, and if that happened . . . . . I had a hunch that they would go against me. Jack, the project manager, was trying hard to keep me in the Distance Learning group, arranging a meeting in my office (instead of a meeting room) . . .

I couldn't think of anything but Tom, and I couldn't think straight. Despite Jack's effort to keep me around the guys, I refused to cooperate, not attending the Distance learning meetings. My mind was so wrapped around Tom, even the possibility of losing my lucky job didn't matter to me. I either had to do something with him or get out, get kicked out since I couldn't quit myself (couldn't walk out on Tom).

Dave came to my office one evening and told me that he could no longer support me. There was a contractor guy who followed Dave, standing outside of my office, looking inside, like he was a cop making sure that Dave would do what he was supposed to do. I was aware that Dave had been getting cornered by many, and he must have gotten cornered to the point of losing everyone if he didn't let go of me. He asked me to check with him after a few months, saying that maybe everything would be okay to bring me back in then, but his voice sounded weak.

Dave walked with me out of the building, and it was raining outside, dark. My mind was blank. Driving back home, I sang several songs loudly, trying not to feel bad about what had just happened.

Self-inflict, Tom said. Self-inflict it was, indeed. I needed to be kicked out to clear my head. I felt lost, but I didn't feel too bad. I learned that people had signed a partition to kick me out, I was the "Christmas Babe!" There was some email about someone turning "pizza-face" at this rally news, must have been John, the HR Head. I felt bad for Tom and very bad for John, for the terrible situation this Christmas Babe rally must have put them into. "Never been so surprised, totally shocked!" Tom said.

They were such great guys who were on top of the world, but they couldn't have a little break that they needed badly. That seemed sad, not fair. Tom Goleniewski was uncomfortable with the fact that I was an Asian. He seemed to have repelled that I appealed to him, wishing to have a White babe, a European, Swedish, white color at least. He needed someone for a little break (pleasure) and I was the closest one he could play a little game with, and this brilliant boss almost got killed for that. How sad!

Kate saved Tom, telling people it was her, not me. She was in love with him or cared for him very much. Not long after I had moved to the Building-1, she had gotten dizzy all of a sudden when she was passing by my cubicle, and she had to sit down for a while to get a hold of herself. When she thought that Tom dumped me after a few months, based on his broadcasted e-mail, she came to visit Linda, my cubicle neighbor, to laugh at me. She was a hefty British-heritage woman, and it was the deepest laugh I had ever heard of, sounding like releasing deep jealousy from her deepest gut.

Tom was devastated that he had no choice but to get stuck with Kate (pretending that it was Kate, not me). He couldn't even say anything to anyone but me, playing Zorro on the Internet, to release his frustration, just enough to be able to breathe. He sent me an e-mail to let me know how frustrated he was, with a disguised ID, or contacted me on the Internet with disguised ID about being stuck with no-baby baby. Kate was a rock, someone who couldn't have intercourse, and her hip looked a little abnormal, uneven, looking like her hips were wobbling a little when she walked. She was a solid woman who understood and supported him well though.

My heart went for Tom and my trust for John . . These Senior Executives could kill for someone who they could relax with every once in a while, without the pressure from her (or anyone), trying to use them to move up the ladder.

I could have prevented the Christmas babe rally, but I let my emotion (not my head) lead the situation. Mr. Zorro kept hovering me on the Internet, sometimes asking me to kick him away, sometimes letting his frustration out a little on me, on someone . .

PART 4
THUMB TAG

SHARPENING MY ENGINEERING SKILLS

This job was more than a sure bet, I thought, but Eric Li, the engineering group manager who interviewed me, was reluctant to bring me in for some reason. Maybe because I acted too confident, overbearing-level, like I owned the DSIA network or the DSIA. Years ago, Dan mentioned to me that I acted like I owned the building when I walked into my contractor's building, doing the GCCS work.

While Eric was dragging his feet, his boss, Ben Rieling, contacted me for another proposal he was getting ready to bid. He was interested in submitting my resume with the bid. After the phone interview, he must have pressured Eric to bring me into the engineering group. In any case, it took over a month for Eric to offer me the position that I thought I was almost too well-qualified, somewhat below my level.

People noticed from the moment I walked into the DSIA Center for Engineering building. Many DSIA people already knew me for my GCCS work, and I felt like I was at home.

Ben Rieling spotted me standing in front of the ACIS engineering area and introduced himself, "You must be Chan, I am Ben Rieling," extending his hand. He was pretty tall, 6'1" or so, gentle but disciplined looking, a good man. His eyes were smiling by the way I looked, I could see.

It was going to be just fine, I thought, and I extended my hand, placing my left hand on top of his hand. He smiled big with his mouth this time, bashfully, and he said he was on his way to a meeting and hurried away ('I gotta play hard to catch'?).

Surprisingly, the team leader was a young female, Kerry, who had been with the group for a year and half, which was the longest time for this group. Other engineers had been with the group for a few months to a year. Kerry was exceptionally sharp, very articulate, and she was working as the lead engineer as well as the trainer. It was a complex network, the largest ATM backbone in the world supporting the US military organizations, and everyone needed to be trained on how the network was operating and what processes were required to perform the various tasks. It was like an ATM boot-camp!

Kerry and another guy, Dennis, who was with ETG, were the only two who could perform the necessary tasks without help. At least they managed to muddle through if they didn't know exactly how to do the task. I vaguely remembered Dennis when I met him, that I met him somewhere before, for some work. And it turned out that he was with the Air Force, stationed in Hawaii, and I had worked with him briefly during the GCCS installation in Hawaii. With that clarification, he became my old-time buddy.

I had been away from the hands-on technical work for a few years, and I needed to sharpen my technical skills along with the training for this specific networking environment. Dennis became my personal trainer and my backup for ETG was subcontracted to ACIS. He was less than thrilled to be my backup, saying, "I am a scummy sub."

I needed to learn quickly since I was hired as one of the senior engineers. Kerry was very supportive of me and more than willing to help me get familiar with this environment. She was a half Korean, and probably that was one of the reasons why she accepted me so well. After a month or so later, I obtained the ATM certification.

DSIA personnel, not just the ATM Services Task Manager but also the engineers, walked into the ACIS work area frequently to ask the ACIS engineers to perform various quick tasks. However, they treated me more like one of them (vs. a contractor) because of my GCCS work, and they were the stronger supporters of me, pushing me as the lead engineer even before I was ready to take the lead.

It was one of the low-end ACIS Groups, an airplane company's IT Sector having merged into the ACIS Federal Communications Group. Just a few White guys and no White guys in the engineering group had the engineering degree. Kerry was a former Air Force, and she didn't have any degree, either. Most members of the engineering/operations support group were minorities, Asians and Blacks, and all of the Asian engineers had the right engineering degree and were part of the engineering group. There was a Vietnamese guy with PhD degree, but his English was hard to understand with everything sounding like *ong-yang-yang*. Some Black engineers had degrees in non-engineering fields, and most Blacks were in the operations support group providing the level-1 support. The subcontractors, ETG with the maintenance contract and Maricon with the ATM support contract, were all White guys, and they were the technical guru's of this DSIA ATM network.

A few months after I joined the group, DSIA and ACIS management started to promote me as the lead engineer. Dennis with ETG and the two ATM experts with Maricon, the ATM switch vendor, were against, supporting Kerry, even getting mad at me (like it was me promoting myself) and calling me the "Dick Head!" The subcontractors were leading ACIS technically, and they had been working closely with Kerry, who was more in their league. I was actually too high for this group overall.

I started to function as the lead engineer for the IP network interfaces, the larger part integrating the customers' networks, and Kerry continued to function as the lead engineer for the ATM core. The DSIA engineer responsible for the IP network interface, Mark, was relatively young, and he seemed pretty pleased with me supporting him, with DSIA people considering me as his partner. His contractors always sent e-mails addressed to "Mark and Chan" and Mark referred me to everyone as the first class lucky babe (12:01/12:07) . . .

ELEVEN

A month after I joined the ACIS ATM group, the DSIA IT Security Manager asked me to help him with his security task (and asked me to be his "eyes and ears" when nobody was around). There was a young guy who didn't like me very much. He stayed mad at me for taking his work space when I first joined the group, and my security task shoot him off! He figured that others would be upset or jealous of me, and he attempted to gang those against me, going around the group, asking "No Chan?"

I had tried to get along well with him, but he kept treating me with *stupid immature arrogance, 'I am the white guy bully' attitude*. With high school education working in the high-tech field as a technician, he had picked up all kinds of bullshits and bad attitudes. He looked like a rebellious, dissatisfied and lazy guy who didn't like to move his body around much, carrying the fat on his stomach like those in 40's or 50's. Every time I tried to talk to him, he crossed his arms and put his foot on his thigh, with no intention of listening to what I had to say. I felt like smacking his head and tell him to do some exercise and lose the stupid fat on his stomach.

Eric's backup, Assistant Manager Gary Conway, didn't like me at first, and I didn't care for him, either, as he looked like a bullish guy with the square jaw. However, he was a shrewd guy and he appreciated my influence with DSIA, promoting me as the ACIS lead engineer. Gary was a stronger manager than Eric, assigning the tasks for engineers, working with the DSIA customers and resolving issues. As soon as I was able to handle the IT interface task without much help, Gary assigned, more like dumped, all of the over-due tasks that had been left behind due to lack of the resources to me, referring me as the "Hot One!"

Gary also assigned me to support the special exercise programs that Dennis used to support. Denis was the most technical guy there, but he was a contractor and besides this MIT graduated ex-military guy didn't care to follow the required Government procedures (paperwork and things) or attending meetings. I was a better communicator, which was the key, and my words had weights with DSIA for my GCCS contribution! Denis was always very helpful, never complained about his privileged task getting turned over to me, just made sarcastic comments every once in a while, like "If you don't know how to do that, just fuck Mark!"

Jon, the most senior guy of the ACIS customer services group, and Gary were the two guys most actively promoted me as the lead engineer and to be the back . . . Jon liked to joke around with me, always teasing me about something and laughing, "It's worth teasing you just looking at the expression on your face." Jon's colleague, another senior member of the group, who appeared to be rather reserved and shy, almost shouted when he saw me, **"Oh, Baby!"** There was a Black guy with the customer services group, and he kept sending e-mails listing my name twice, "Chan Chan" (implying that they could use two of me there).

Eric referred Kerry as a daughter and me as a son (11), and later he said, after Kerry left ACIS to join the Maricon, "We have the sun and the moon at the same place." He seemed rather goofy, a typical Chinese guy in America, making goofy Chinese-like comments, I thought. He usually kept his position neutral, staying away from me, never asking me to do anything or trying to promote me. When others supported me, he didn't go against me, just quietly consented, more or less.

I sent out an e-mail asking Mr. Rieling's direction (123/321), and his response was 321, and with that, I was the back, officially, for the group, and he was 319 . . . Everyone seemed okay with that for a while, but some people started to backfire . . . .

DEALING WITH TROUBLE MAKERS

Ben Rieling, the ACIS Task Manager, didn't interact with engineers much. His office was located far away from the ACIS engineering group's work area, and he was frequently away from the building to his ACIS office.

Two managers under Ben, Steve and Jeff, the old airplane company managers packaged with the merge to ACIS, worked more closely with the engineers, with their office located at the ACIS engineering area. They both looked like high-level managers; Steve looked like a tough boss, good-looking, and Jeff seemed like a stuck-up hypo, looking like a guy who should live in one of the New England states.

ACIS and the subcontractors were supporting the DSIA network as on-site contractors, and we didn't have the most comfortable work space. Steve, Jeff, and another old airplane company's managers were sharing an office. I was sharing a work space with five other engineers, including Kerry and the bullish pain-in-the-neck young guy, Keith.

I had been trying to move away from Keith, who was constantly playing little games to annoy me. He kept changing the order of the names posted next to the door, placing my name at the bottom, below the subcontractor guy who was sharing the same space, kept putting half-emptied soda bottle or other stupid little things on my desk.

Enough was enough. I didn't need to have to put up with his annoying game. I asked Ben to find me another work space, and while he was looking for a space to move me in, DSIA provided a new office for Steve and Jeff. Steve passed his old office to me, and with that, people started gossiping about him and me..

On one Thursday, Jeff came by, apparently trying to hook up with me, playing with his fingers (52-). I never cared for him very much, and I was pretty irritated by his behavior but pretended that I didn't catch what he was trying.. I just politely talked about the task he came to see me to clarify. Later, he came by and took my whiteboard. It was the old Steve's whiteboard, and maybe he was sharing that stupid whiteboard with Steve as well. What a cheapie!! He was going to be a pain in the ass, the little bully kind that I can't stand!! He was tall and looked like a classy guy, acting rather stuck-up as if he was higher than everyone else. A cheap hypo kind, obviously, with strong racial attitude.

Later, Jon, the playful customer services guy, came by and said to my officemate, another old airplane company manager who left out, "Keep her down!" Apparently, Jeff was out to get me, to either make me his babe or kick me out!!--.

Eric was just focusing on getting the work done, but with all this pick-up's going on, he must have thought that he should try as well. After all, he was my direct manager holding my paycheck. He came to my office one evening, after everyone in the same office had gone, and he was putting his one foot on a chair sitting near my desk. This goofy and nervous manager didn't measure the height of the chair correctly and stumbled, hopping back with his one foot on the ground. I had to hold my lips tight not to laugh, looking away. He figured he looked like an amateur, and mumbled something about the task I was working on and left quickly.

Steve and some DSIA people were interested in switching the ACIS engineering management from <Eric and Gary> to <Gary and Chan>. Eric was not a bad manager. He retired from the Marine Corp as a Lieutenant Colonel and probably had strong military leadership trainings. He was the only Asian manager I had seen, which surprised me when I first met him, judging by the way he looked. He didn't look like an elite, looked more like a grocery store owner or someone doing some kind of hard/physical work.

The HR manager called me and asked me to meet her to talk about the work environment at DSIA facility. We met at Ben's office, and she told me to contact her if I needed any help, but she was not interested in helping me. My instinct told me that she wanted to find an excuse she could use against me.

One day, Jeff and Eric asked me in for a meeting. Apparently, someone, probably Jeff, had contacted HR manager and informed her about me1, cornering Eric. And Eric probably was mad at me for being in the position of running him over with Gary and went along with Jeff. They had written up a list of rules that I needed to follow.

One of the items on the list was not to contact Ben, and they pressured me to sign this paper. What they were trying to do was totally ridiculous, but I didn't feel like (didn't have much chance) arguing with these two ridiculous managers who were trying to over-exercise their power over me.. The HR manager, a bullish chubby woman who didn't like me, was not going to be on my side, one way or another, for sure. Nothing gained arguing with a manager who was determined to be a pain for being rejected and the HR manager who'd rather not have me work there in the first place, I could figure. I had no choice but to sign it. The HR manager was interested in cornering Ben and Steve, to exercise her power over them, it looked like. And Jeff (and Eric) got the HR manager's help competing against Ben and Steve, trying to get me.. Men (959)!!

Sure enough, Jeff came to my office soon after, joking with the old airplane company manager sharing the office with me, "It's a paw-less rabbit now. Ha Ha Ha~" What an asshole! Ben found out about this HR-overpowering action later and sent out an e-mail, reprimanding them meekly.

Gary's wife joined the group, as a member of the configuration management group, to help with the paperwork and maintaining the process databases. She was a housewife with no experience in the professional world. At first, Gary asked the engineers to use her to help with the tedious low-level paperwork, working from home as a part-time helper, and a few months later, he was able to bring his wife into the group.

She was a coarse looking, totally unpolished as a professional. She seemed to be afraid of me at first, avoiding the eye contact with me and bending away at the sight of me as quickly as she could. Then after a few weeks, she became ridiculously brave, referring me as a hole or whatever as she was becoming friendly with Kerry, who was sharing an office with me. 'Geez, why do I need to put up with this inferior-attack?' I just rolled my eyes when she picked in her head into my office to talk to Kerry (to bitch about me).

In the engineering meetings, Gary's wife kept touching Gary like she was at home, to remind everyone that he was her husband! Everyone was getting bad taste in their mouths for her unprofessional behaviors, but they put up with her, trying not to stir up an uncomfortable situation with Gary.

Gary changed his attitudes towards me with his wife around. It was more like he was trying to stay away from me, just doing the minimum interactions necessary to get the work done, often looking embarrassed. He needed his wife to bring extra income to raise his children, and his wife wasn't just doing the work quietly but was trying to position herself as his equal. Gary had over 20 years of experience and she had just started. It was totally outrageous (and ignorant of her), and I asked Ben Rieling, disgusted, "Did you consent to hire Gary's wife?"

Dan had joined another DSIA networking group as a ACIS contractor, working at a different building located nearby. He often came to the DSIA Center for Engineering building for meetings and stopped by my office. My office mate, an old airplane company manager handling the hardware procurement, was one of the guys who thought I was too much (too much for him, that is), however, he seemed to like Dan and became friendly whenever Dan came to see me . . . Dan always had quietly good manners smoothing people around me . . .

Dealing with people at this level, being modest would not be treated as a merit. These people would just try to step all over me if I tried to be modest, thinking that I was humble for being an Asian, a scared minority to abuse. Being humble can only shine with one's position or with those who recognize that virtue. Self promotion, in a subtle way, would be a better way to deal with people at work, for a better environment, with more confident people. Dealing with unreasonable troublemakers with negative intention, the best thing I could do was to ignore what they tried to do if at all possible and to stay away from them.

DOG-EAT-DOG RAT RACE

One day, I raised my voice on Eric for not providing directions for new network upgrade plan, which I had to provide some answers to DSIA customers. Next day, I got a call from the HR manager requesting a consultation. Gary's wife had witnessed the scene, called the HR manager and told her how I was arrogant and unprofessional, showing no respect for my manager. Geez, please!

The bullish woman HR manager, referring Eric as "Mr. Li," which made me want to puke, jumped up and down on me for my behavior. She probably was bored, and what a chance to kick me around that phone call must have been! Eric didn't have any problem with my behavior. He understood the situation and apologized for the bad situation that I had to deal with, due to no direction from the management. It was a boot-camp environment lacking directions.

When Ben said that I was the back, with him 19, everyone seemed to be okay with that. Nobody said anything against. One senior Black operator behaved badly at first, playing with his pants when I visited the Operations Center, but he cooled down quickly, with my 'YOU IDIOT!' look. He actually became friendlier and started to pass the level 3 operational support work to me after that.

DSIA signed 9-year extended ATM Services Contract with Ben . . . . Then one day, I asked a Black guy, a DSIA employee doing the security-related work, to go to lunch with me. He seemed like a reasonable guy, and I needed someone to have lunch with, no-strings-attached, no sexual or any kind of tension, just a friend. I felt comfortable with Mark, but he was the customer who I was supporting, and with him, it could be more like a date, the power lunch date with an important customer. When I ran into Mark at the cafeteria, he said, "Looks like you need someone to have lunch with more than I do." I didn't need any kind of unnecessary tension or distracting gossips, and this Black guy seemed like a good person for having a simple lunch with.

Next thing I knew was that this seemingly cool and reserved Black guy broadcasted an e-mail implying himself as 19, and the Black people were dancing in front of my office. Soon after, the DSIA Senior Executives came down to my office area, looking at me, looked disgusted and puzzled. 'Really, What the hell is this nonsense all about?,' I was thinking myself. That was NOT good.

Time for me to move on . . . I contacted an ACIS VP, an Australian-American, a friend of Jerry, who was in the process of establishing an engineering office in Australia. He said it would take some time before he could bring me in, and he would let me know when he was ready to get a new project started in Australia. I was very interested in the possibility of working in another country, having seen what could happen, but I couldn't wait for him to hire me for his venture.

I needed a job that I could start immediately, possibly to flee out of the country to avoid becoming a crushed yellow-shrimp. I had not worked with many Blacks and had never thought about how a little thing like having a lunch with a Black guy could turn into a suffocating racial situation until this incident, getting twisted into the racial ego-play generating suffocating atmosphere!

The Black guys who I worked with in this job were fine, except a Black secretary guy supporting Ben. He was a pain abusing the email-broadcasting against me, trying to exercise his stupid secretary THE power over me. A more experienced higher-level Black guy with the Customer Support group, Leed, was very supportive of me, even actively promoting me with "Chan Chan" e-mails. Leed came to see me, too, thrilled by what was going on, and I didn't know how to tell him that it was a twisted blow-up of another Black guy.

It was a case of Blacks turning my 316 status into a racial matter, and it was terrible. They could have used several Chans, really, but instead, everyone was fighting over one Chan . . . .

PART 5
BRAIN WORK

WORKING ON RESEARCH PROJECT

I posted my resume on the Monster.com as usual, but this time, I wasn't getting many responses. Just a few small companies contacted me with various positions. The overall response was totally different from the last time, and in most cases, the recruiters turned me down without passing my resume to the hiring manager, for one reason or another. Some were just contacting me out of curiosity. I was getting nervous about my job situation, and I responded to an unknown company, IPT, located in Boston area.

An IPT project manager in Washington DC area, Chris Mcguire who interviewed me was very nice and polite, even compassionate about me trying to join a small company, after having worked for a prestigious company like Karlmon Dietech supporting business development work. The recruiter, Jan, came down to meet with me and gave me a business card of her boss, the president of the company, Chi Hwang, and I was pleasantly surprised. Chris was a former Air Force, doing an Air Force database modernization project, and he and Jan offered me the position at the spot.

A former offer letter came within a week as the Program Manager supporting an ACIS research project, with a small salary cut. My task sounded very challenging, almost too challenging. It was more than I had bargained for, and I joined the IPT without thinking twice.

I was to report to an ACIS project manager, Andy Dennison, located at a seven storage building shared by several IT integration companies. I reported there on Monday morning, and the ACIS hadn't prepared a work space for me. Another IPT program manager, an old guy in his 70's, brought me a computer to the conference room that I was to use temporarily. It almost looked like the ACIS people there were going to test me first, before allowing me in . . . Some people were speculating, anyway.

Nobody introduced me to Andy Dennison, and I went into his office to introduce myself and to get started on the project. He looked like a quick-witted guy with sparkling eyes, a naughty kind. I didn't have the foggiest idea of how the IPT presented me to the ACIS or to this Andy guy. He seemed to think that I was a knucklehead, walking into his office with my notebook and asking him questions about the project. He was reluctant to answer my questions, giving me short answers with '*What the hell does this crazy Asian girl think she is doing here, questioning me with things that she does not need to know!?*' attitude. Maybe he didn't know the answers in details. In any case, he looked irritated like I was bothering him, doing unnecessary things. So I made it short.

Three days after I joined the group, ACIS had their intermediate briefing to the MDO customers. Andy's lead engineer, Mari, asked me to join the briefing. There were five of us to go to the MDO at the Pentagon for the briefing, and they were talking about whether to take one car or two. I didn't think I would be much of a help with little knowledge of the project, and I said I would remain at the office. I assumed Andy didn't care for me going to the Pentagon based on his attitude when I introduced myself. Surprisingly, Andy insisted that I should attend the briefing to learn what was going on with this project, and he would take another car.

MDO customers were very dissatisfied with what the ACIS presented, and some even walked out in the middle of the briefing. I could see why, I couldn't even follow the ACIS presentation myself. What the ACIS presented was too abstract, totally confusing. It looked like they tried to develop the technology roadmaps without the knowledge of the MDO communities' operating environment. After the briefing, Andy introduced me to the customer as a new member who just joined the group, with a slight hope that I might be able to turn this failing situation around. Something needed be changed. Otherwise, they would lose the project in no time.

On our way back to the office, I was riding with Andy and Mari, and I recommended they would need to analyze the MDO communities' current operating environment first and use that as the ground. When we returned to the office, Andy, embarrassed by their failure, dropped his ACIS badge on the floor. He was definitely more expressive than I initially thought, not necessarily speaking his thoughts out.

The old IPT program manager moved to another office closer to his project group, and I moved into his office. It was arranged to have me sitting at the back center looking at the door, and my engineer, a retired Marine pilot, was sitting at a corner with his back-head towards me. It was rather awkward having to look at the back of his head all the time, and as for him, he seemed to feel embarrassed about me being his new boss watching the back of his head.

The ACIS provided me with survey reports and some data they had collected, as I requested. Each survey report was just 3-4 pages, each one with different information. Apparently, they had met with various site representatives randomly who were willing to cooperate with them and collected whatever the site representatives could provide them with. No survey template, no consistency of the data collected from each site.

I brought in a survey template that I had developed for my GCCS task, which was over 80 pages, and showed it to Andy telling him that this was the kind of document we needed to collect the site information, to develop the technology roadmaps that the MDO customer had requested. Andy seemed to be in a shock, but he joked, "We need more than 3-4 pages, huh? Ha ha~" Then he ran out with my survey template, looking like he had seen a ghost or something. Where was he going with that?

I analyzed the data that the ACIS had collected and tasked my engineer, the ex-Marine pilot, to determine what information was missing for developing the technology roadmaps. He didn't come up with anything, but he kept bringing popcorns to the office instead, holding the popcorns high up.

Mr. Marine Pilot had been supporting this project for several months before I joined the group, and the ACIS expressed dissatisfaction about him not having made enough contribution to the project. I developed a list of missing information studying various document and asked this incompetent Marine pilot to find another position that matched his background better.

Andy had another contractor, Miltech, located in Huntsville, Alabama, and the Program Manager was a single blonde, Stacy. Stacy was leading this research task, and she got annoyed when I informed everyone what the missing information was to develop the roadmap and what needed to be done, asking her to come up to Washington DC to discuss the plan to move forward. Perhaps I sounded too bossy or made her feel less than competent, unintentionally. She responded to my e-mail implying to *flush* something (as in flushing toilet, trying to put me down, obviously).

Stacy came up, and we talked for a while in my office. She tried to be supportive of what I intended to do, then she went to work with Mari. Stacy and Mari worked together for a week, while I was sitting in my office by myself, reviewing the document. I heard Andy asking them to invite me to their working sessions, but they never did. I didn't ask them to include me, either, since I needed time to catch up myself, reviewing what they had done and reviewing a bunch of DoD architecture standard documents.

I hired a new engineer, Rick Smith, who I knew from my DSIA ATM work. Rick was with ETG then, working with Dennis. Rick was a tall, easy-going, good-looking guy who everyone liked. I let him use my desk, instead of having to put up with the awkward seating, and I worked from home. A few weeks later, some of the people in the suite moved out, and I asked Andy to give us another office. It was a super treatment for Rick, but he was reluctant to move to one of the vacant offices, trying to keep my office as his. He was testing my patience, probably thinking that he might be able to jerk me around. I told him get his butt out of my office!

Sometimes Andy walked by my office with electronic gadgets, making some "pyong-pyong" or "te-ong te-ong sounds. In addition to playing with his little gadgets, he played pin-ball game frequently, making a lot of ball noises. Nobody else seemed to play the pin-ball game. It was probably his idea to setup the pin-ball game room. He was like a naughty little boy, holding the VP title.

The next office to mine was occupied by a White female, Monica, who was a PAIN. She had a fast big mouth, always talking a lot and talking fast. She was not a member of my project team, yet she kept sticking her head in to Andy's office to babble with him, her boss, when we were having a team meeting. She stood at the door and babbled forever about things that had no relation to our project. Andy usually had to tell her that he needed to continue with his meeting. Otherwise, I asked her to talk to Andy after the meeting when I was out of my patience before Andy, after listening to her babbling endlessly, for 20-30 minutes.

Monica didn't like me very much, of course, and she kept slamming her office door when she was leaving every evening. She slammed the door so hard that the sound always startled me! Dr. Moore, a Program Manager located in Pennsylvania, said at the first conference call with me, "My condolence for sitting next to Monica." She was an extremely self-centered female and even bitched to Andy about me being too confident, "She is s~o sure of herself."

At the office across from mine were two female software engineers, developing programs as contractors to the ACIS for some other project. One was an Indian and the other was a Chinese, and both of them were relatively young. The Indian female was friendlier, smiling at me at least, but the Chinese female was avoiding an eye contact with me (or with anyone).

Other people in the building started to notice me, making pleased comments with smiles when they saw me, "We got the cell-phone?" I didn't know I was supposed to be some kind of cell-phone? Then I heard some women mentioning a "hot dog" in the building.

One day, the Chinese female across my office had put out the lunch-bag formed like a huge dick! Andy and other ACIS people were laughing at that, looking at each other with amusement, thinking 'What an idiot!' "Idiot!" I said towards her office, and she or maybe her office mate played, "You've got the male" recording. A few days later, the Chinese female had her long hair cut down short.

Andy was a light guy with thin ears, or just a fast acting manager, and every time someone said something about me, he seemed to get nervous. He was nervous about me himself, and he sent e-mails in red-and-blue, trying to warn people of me (or as a warning to me, being too advanced) sometimes. He displayed some kind of status concerning me in his trash can sitting outside of his office. He was intrigued by me, walking by my office frequently to check what I was doing, and his eyes lighted up when I looked up to see him walking by . .

One day, I was standing behind my desk, and I must have had my hands on my waist without realizing, just trying to figure out what needed to be worked on, and saw Andy walking by. He looked absolutely impressed by me standing there, looking like a total boss! (Dan had told me how he was impressed by my posture with my hands on my waist before).

I often ran into Andy in the kitchen area alone, and when that happened, he became shy, barely mumbling to respond to what I said to him, which would be just a small talk acknowledging him being there. Apparently, he had never dealt with someone like me, and he seemed thrilled, and at the same time, annoyed and nervous.

Andy did all kinds of things, sending all kinds of sounds from his office using his electronic gadgets or PC. He even walked around holding his hands up high, forming his hands like he was carrying a bowl, implying my status. He had some kind of crush on me, I thought, or maybe he just needed some fun-break, just like others (younger or older, higher or lower, brainy or idiotic), from his daily dry work or the monotonous marriage life.

LEADING NETWORK ARCHITECTURE DEVELOPMENT

Andy's project group was full of females. Mari, his lead engineer for this project was a female, who was very nice but seemed to be a little off, somehow. His other contractor, Stacy and everyone under her were females. I was a female. Andy and Rick were the only guys in this project team, and Andy scratched his arms and legs, left and right, up and down, like crazy, whenever we were in meeting or conference calls. His backup manager was also a woman, a very spunky woman, not to mention the blabber-mouth fat babe, Monica.

I had had enough of this fat babe slamming the door! One day, when Andy was out, I walked in and out of my office every half an hour, slamming the door hard every time, to get back to her. When Andy came back to his office, she ran to him to report that I was either drugged or gone crazy. Andy didn't say anything, and she left, mumbling she needed to get away from my madness.

A few days later, I couldn't open my office door. Someone had locked it, probably Monica, who was carrying a bunch of keys around. It was very annoying and I felt like smacking her head, but she wasn't around. Andy giggled like it was a fun, "Oh, someone locked your door?"

The team had agreed to develop a survey template, and I developed a Table of Content of the site survey template to collect the information needed for implementing the modeling & simulation collaboration environment for the MDO sites. I asked Rick if he could lead the survey template development instead of me, understanding how others might feel if I did. He needed some time to catch up, he said, so I led the effort of developing the first few sections, and everyone was very enthusiastic and supportive, to my surprise.

Stacy came up every once in a while to incorporate her team's work. An old IPT program manager saw Andy and Stacy leaving the building going out to lunch and he looked worried, like I am failing my mission there, like I got dumped (or didn't get favored by Andy), and we would get funding cut. When I first joined the group, he thanked Jan, the HR, for sending me, CHAN, to this group. I just shrugged like I couldn't care less.

Andy had been working with Stacy for a long time, and besides, she was a visitor. No big deal. She was a fairly good-looking blonde, but I didn't consider her as my competition. She looked professional but somewhat trashy looking, I thought, with long hair hanging down, the overall mood. I was pretty sure that Andy was fascinated by me, doing all kinds of things to get my attention. I had called Andy once when I couldn't make the regular meeting, and later I heard him telling Monica that I sounded like a scratch on the phone (but other than that, I was perfect).

Besides helping Rick leading the survey template development, I was developing the network architecture myself. I showed my diagrams to an ACIS engineer, who was working on a different project, flirting with him,

"The one and only masterpiece done by Chan!" He was the nicest guy there who often came in to my office to chat with me, "Wow, the cloud within the cloud, pretty impressive" . . .

This group was much higher-level than the other ACIS group that I was with supporting the DSIA ATM services, and I was thankful for not having to deal with the difficult situation arising from the level difference (lower level hating the higher level, etc.), certainly nothing close to the Black and White situation I had experienced. Everyone, except Monica, was pretty nice, and the only Black guy engineer for this group was super nice. Andy's secretary, an old Black woman, was friendly and helpful, not like those Karlmon Dietech secretaries who wanted to play the babe for their bosses (and hated me).

Rick kept suggesting me to have sex with him putting his knee on the table. When he did, I just looked at his posture unmoved. He kept me a good company for lunch, and sometimes, for drinks after work. He was a super easy-going nice guy and I felt very comfortable with him, but I kept the distance. Sometimes he tried to overpower me, and I had to threaten him that I would fire him if he didn't behave correctly. I was the brain, and I was mentoring him to become a lead engineer. It was a jump from the operations support technician to work on a high-level research project, a chance I offered him because he was a White guy. A chance that nobody would have offered me if I were a technician with high-school education.

Rick did appreciate me and treated me well most of the time. Every once in a while his White male ego seemed to be creeping up on him. When that happened, he acted like a jerk trying to put me down with some ridiculous gestures, putting his butt up high on the air and doing things like that. Nevertheless, Rick turned out to be an excellent asset to my task, pleasing everyone.

The team developed a comprehensive professional survey template with my guidance and modified the abstract roadmaps, and I also developed a network architecture to present to the MDO. The technology roadmaps were still pretty abstract with no real data as we didn't have enough information to use as the ground. It required more resources (more funding) to study and analyze the MDO's current operating environment.

MDO funded for the subsequent research on Wednesday at 4:00 o'clock, Andy told me, and he introduced me to another ACIS manager who would be working with me for the subsequent task, without the Miltech. I had become fairly close to Stacy and had talked to her more frequently than the ACIS engineers, but her modeling and simulation expertise was no longer needed for new network security task. I practically saved ACIS for this task, besides bringing in the energy . . . .

My contribution was vital for getting the subsequent funding, and I consulted with Chi about raising the IPT labor rate. He was thrilled and was able to raise my rate by 7% and Rick's rate by 4%. Rick really didn't deserve to have a raise since he hadn't done anything exceptional, just carrying on the engineering work with my help. Chi thought the salary I offered to Rick was too high to begin with, considering his background.

Andy wasn't happy with me raising the rate, giving me the pretty darn annoyed look, calling me "Turkey!" Nevertheless, he assigned Mari to support me with the new task that I was leading. Andy seemed to have a crush on me, yet he hated me being a shrewd Program Manager.

My new task was to study the viability of using the public Internet for MDO classified data. David, an ACIS networking group manager, had a few meetings with the NSA but had not produced any result. It was for providing the backup connection for the MDO communities, the 2nd priority task, however, due to the security requirement, it was a more difficult, higher-level task.

For my first task, I tried hard to prove myself as an asset, a responsible and useful subcontractor, jumping in to provide my comments as quickly as possible. When I was the first one to make comments, some ACIS managers got annoyed, and immediately, two of them sent me "out-of-office" auto-reply timed at 5:36 and 5:44 (not an automated reply). I was a subbie, and my goal was to support and please the prime managers and get the most funding possible . . . I never jumped first to make comments after that. Be helpful, but try not to lead or outshine the prime unless necessary, I learned my lesson.

I had been sitting around for a month waiting for the ACIS management to provide me with the status of this project and some directions (as I had learned not to initiate the discussion). I needed to be careful not to look like I was more responsible for getting started and making the progress. I started my e-mail, "Hello, is anybody awake? My face is turning blue holding my breath, waiting for your directions . . . ."

I heard Andy Dennison laughing first, and later, his boss, Dr. Moore, responded to my e-mail, in navy . . . 'PhD, playing too, huh' I thought and thought I'd better play his game, and I responded in blue. He responded in purple, I responded in olive, he responded in grey, I responded in hunter green, and he responded in hunter green.. The work got started with Dr. Moore arranging a conference call with his team.

A new woman moved to this office suite from another ACIS group, a middle-aged chunky woman with a darker skin, maybe a Spanish-American. I didn't know what her responsibility was, couldn't care-less. Then a few days later, she said out of blue, almost shouting *"Yellow doesn't need an office!"* walking by my office. The whole suite got very quiet. Andy was in his office, but he was like he wasn't even breathing.

I asked Jerry for an advice, if I should make an issue out of her crazy comment, and his advice was to consult with her boss. Her boss, Andy, just got nervous, but Jerry couldn't have known that.

Something needed to be done to correct her ridiculously brave comment like she was doing the right thing. I walked over to her office and asked her, "Did you hear someone saying *yellow doesn't need an office*? I know it wasn't Monica or Mari. I recognize their voice. I couldn't recognize the voice." She looked surprised by my direct confrontation, saying, "Some said that? I didn't hear anything." And I said, staring at her, "Yes, someone did say that, and I am trying to find out who would make such a ridiculous comment! If you hear about it, would you let me know?" And she mumbled, "Sure." I asked her about her previous work to figure out what kind of person would say such a thing directly, like an idiot, as Jerry stated. She was a former Karlmon Dietech employee, she said. That must have been where her spunk came from, but obviously she was too stupid or too unpolished for that classic Company, I figured.

The DISN-LES was holding a networking conference at the JPO building, and I couldn't miss it, even being so close. I sat in the middle row, and John, one of my old DSIA friends, was looking back at me, smiling. I was glad to see him there, wondering, 'Why is he here? He is not into networking.' I looked around the room to see that attendees were all guys, except a few females representing DSIA, and I was the only Asian at the conference.

The contractor program manager for the DISN-LES seemed to have some problem with me attending this conference, acting nervous and kept giving me annoyed look when he was presenting the DISN-LES project status. Then the next presenter, the JPO Director, also kept looking at me when he was giving the briefing, every few seconds, and some guy joked about "4-plane going" with him . . . . All the guys were laughing at his comment . . . That made me uncomfortable. The only people who I knew in the room were John and a guy with the Mitre who supported some GCCS task.

For the lunch break, John came to me and said, "You're still making trouble, huh?" The JPO Director saw John and me going out to lunch together, and John looked very proud, wanting to tell the Director, 'I already got her' . . .

It turned out that John was working at a JPO building as a DSIA liaison supporting the DISN-LES, and I often had lunch with him since his office was within the walking distance. I was interested in introducing Jerry and John, for possible business opportunities for Jerry (and possibly to develop a new project for me), however, both of them were reluctant and I was waiting for an appropriate business opportunity to introduce the two.

In the meantime, I introduced Jerry and Chris, an IPT project manager, inviting Jerry to the IPT office where Chris was located, to have them discuss the possible subcontract opportunities. Jerry was doing the business development for the SDE, the largest IT integrator, and Chris was very interested in the project opportunity with the SDE.

Jerry and Chris talked for an hour, discussing various projects that SDE might need a subcontractor for, then we went out to have lunch at a very upscale restaurant. I seldom went to a nice restaurant for lunch, usually going to places like Chilli or Ruby Tuesday level, but these two men were too much of businessmen for a place like that. Ruby Tuesday was perfect for having lunch with Dan, with a few drinks, joking around . . .

ACIS provided me with a 500 sq ft office/work space at their Towers. It was to be shared with Rick and for setting up a small lab that I needed for my task. I didn't measure it but Andy told me it was 500 sq ft, and it was big enough to dance around, really. Apparently, ACIS people at the Towers had heard about me, referring me as "once in a lifetime catch."

I met with Dr. Moore, Andy, and David to discuss my new task, and David suggested that we develop a security specification matrix. I had telephone conferences with Dr. Moore, but it was the first time I met him. He didn't look like a PhD, looked more like a low level technician or a construction worker, and I was uncomfortable with him face-to-face. David was reluctant to join this meeting, thinking that Dr. Moore had a thing for me, but he did come to the meeting half an hour late and came out as the winner to work with me, instead of Dr. Moore.

David and I drafted a networking architecture with possible security functionalities needed. His office was in Maryland, and he visited my office once a month to discuss the progress and issues. David was a relatively young manager, somewhat intimated by me, and I tried to keep myself below his level, not to outshine him (embarrass him). Otherwise, he might be uncomfortable to work with me.

Rick and I met with the leading firewall and intrusion detection system vendors to obtain the evaluation copy of their systems. These product vendors' account managers and sales engineers didn't know that I was the program manager and Rick was working for me. I always asked Rick to arrange the meetings with the vendors and waited for him to ask a question first, making it look like he was the lead engineer and I was supporting him. They always figured out that I was a higher-level during the discussion, of course. Rick and Mari evaluated the security systems and developed a security specification matrix with my guidance. I turned the security specification matrix over to David to present it to the MDO.

ACIS didn't invite me (IPT) for the final briefing to the MDO. After the briefing, the ACIS informed Chi Hwang that they had 60% funding reduction for the 3rd phase of the project and they would not be able to fund the IPT for the subsequent task.

PROJECT DEVELOPMENT

Chi came down to Washington DC with a new business development guy, Tim, who retired from ACIS. Tim and I talked about the possible project opportunities for me, and he was making me nervous by kept looking at me with dirty eyes. It was hot, and I was sweating, literally. He needed to use me to bring in some work, presenting me to larger companies possibly as a back support to them, not to drool over me himself!

Tim called me after the meeting, trying to pressure me to be his babe (without Chi, his Chinese boss-, watching him), acting like he was doing me a favor since he was going to bring in some work for me. It was going to be a pain to work with him. I kept my position professional, trying not to get caught in any kind of awkward situation, just trying to keep good working relationship with him.

Tim was not a well-educated guy, judging by the way he wrote e-mails, which sounded like a guy with high-school education with bad grade in English. He probably worked as a technician throughout his career, not doing much writing. Most engineers need to write technical document and have fairly good writing skills developed. He kept sending e-mails in navy, kept pressuring me to be his babe, in coarse manners.

I pretended that I wasn't getting what he was trying to do with me for a while, then I decided to correct this annoying situation. I forwarded his e-mail to Chi, but I soon realized that it was a mistake. What could Chi do? I just made him feel awkward with his business development guy who was much older, possibly over-powering Chi, for him being a high-level Asian. Jan, the HR, was already over-powering Chi in some ways, acting like she was THE president. In fact, most of the IPT employees, the White guys mostly, didn't treat Chi as the president, and Jan was covering him.

I needed Jerry to help me out of this situation and introduced Tim to Jerry to work on the project opportunity with SDE. Tim didn't invite me for his meeting with SDE that Jerry had arranged with their Program Managers, which he should have. I kept supporting Tim to develop the project opportunity with SDE. If he succeeded, I would be working at the SDE facility, and I could put up with his annoying manners for that.

In the meantime, I contacted other companies and various ACIS groups for possible project opportunities, but everyone was cold. Most of the program managers, directors, and VPs were White guys, and they weren't interested in signing even a small subtask with me regardless how qualified I was for the task. Some of them tried to bring me into their companies as a back support instead, but it went nowhere. Parachuting only made everyone cold. Jerry connected me with a Black Program Manager, but he didn't even respond to me.

Chi paid me for a few months while I was trying to bring a project in, but he couldn't afford to continue to pay my salary without additional funding source. I wasn't ready to give up yet, and I kept trying every program managers, directors, and VP's. Nobody was interested in even checking the possibility of signing a contract, even a tiny potion, with me, or developing a possible project with me.

I contacted Mike Pucillo with DSIA for a project opportunity listed on the DSIA contract opportunity site, and thankfully, he suggested me to prepare a proposal for setting up a GIG task related lab. Finally, I was getting somewhere. It was exciting, and I was counting the money since I would get the percentage of the contract if I succeeded.

I contacted Ben Rieling, the ACIS ATM Task Manager, for his advice and recommendation, and he linked me with one of the ACIS Program Manager, Bill. I had a high hope for this DSIA project opportunity, but Bill somebody never responded to me, despite Ben's recommendation.

So much for my high hope. I shoot an e-mail to Rob, an ACIS network engineer, who supported the largest DoD network before Dan did. Rob was visiting Ft. Monmouth, NJ, supporting a DSIA exercise program, and a week later, I visited Rob's office at the ACIS Towers. He was a good-looking guy, almost PhD, dragging his feet for writing the dissertation. He was motivated enough to pursue the PhD degree but not motivated enough. At his professional stage, the PhD degree would not make much difference anyway.

Rob wasn't really interested in working on the project opportunity that I contacted him for, but he was interested in bringing me in for his voice communications project for DSIA. I had little experience with the voice communications, and Rob was reluctant to give me a new chance.

Dan knew that I was meeting with Rob, and he was waiting for me in front of my condo. I was mad at Dan for not helping me with the DSIA project opportunity (I did ask him first, of course), and I had ignored him when he contacted me to chat on the Internet. He must have worried that Rob might become my new best friend, and he couldn't bear that. Rob was a cute guy, and I needed someone who could work with me. I snapped at Dan for coming to my place without my consent, and he left looking sad with his head down.

One of the DSIA engineers who just got transferred to the GIG-BE project acquisition office told me that he would consider using me as an on-site contractor. When I first contacted him, his response was "ummmm, maybe." A few days later, I called him again, sometime after 5 o'clock, and his voice got elated with positive response, "Could you send me the document and give me some time to review?"

It would take a while to get the contract vehicle to work as an on-site contractor, but I needed to start at somewhere. While I was working on my next step, I discovered that some other small company had already had the contract supporting the same task as an on-site contractor and they were looking for help. It was Dan who found out about this contract playing golf with another DSIA engineer, and he suggested me to contact the lead engineer for this contract. I knew that I would be too much, however, Dan advised me that I should mould myself to fit in. I sent my resume to this lead engineer, and Dan was calling me from a bar asking me to join him for a drink, all happy, telling me that he told this lead engineer that I was a "God-sent babe!" Despite Dan's effort, this lead engineer guy got intimated by my background and shied away.

The first DSIA GIG-BE Industry Conference was held on Friday, October 11, at the DSIA Skyline facility. The registration started at 7:30am, and when I got there, there was a long line of attendees getting their name tags and going through the security check. The guard at the door smiled at me when I entered the door, like he knew who I was.

The conference room was full with over 300 attendees representing various IT companies who were holding DoD contracts or were interested in becoming the DoD contractors. The front row was mostly DSIA employees scheduled to give briefings or those helping the briefers and the attendees. I looked around the room, full of guys, and I sat in the back row quietly, trying not to get noticed. Some guy sitting near me made a comment to a guy next to him as I was sitting down, "She is the queen, huh?"

DSIA distributed the conference document, and I skimmed through, checking the attendees list. Most of the attendees were program managers or directors. I registered myself as a program manager for IPT, but I felt like I was a little off representing IPT, whose business focus was far away from this large network backbone work. Nevertheless, I was confident that I would be one of the better qualified persons for this project, if not the best qualified person.

The conference was to present the first part of the DoD integration network transformation effort to provide OC-192 backbone implementing the optical switching. I knew the DSIA Program Director from my GCCS years. I didn't know him personally, but I knew who he was (what he did), which was a step ahead than most people in the room.

I had tried to talk to Dave Turgeon, my old Karlmon Dietech boss, about supporting me with this DSIA project, to check the possibility of bringing this project into Karlmon Dietech. I needed to find out more details to convince him if it was worth the shot.

The conference covered DSIA's strategic plans, transformation roadmap, program overview, acquisition plans, and various other issues. I took many notes as a front-runner of this project while others were just listening. After the conference, I contacted numerous people on the list to check the possibility of working on this global network standardization and integration project, to get a piece, but I learned that I was just running on empty.

I always got my job by responding, never by pursuing, however, I had no choice but aggressively pursuing project opportunities. I needed to be responsive to survive in this male-dominated field, not aggressive, and I knew I hit the glass-ceiling for myself.

Detailed Egg Report

PART 6

REBUILDING TIME

E-mail collection

Lt Gen Strickler:

Lt Col Doyle advised me not to send you personal e-mail, but I feel that I need to explain the situation and why I've asked you for help.

I have no intention of causing you any trouble or put you in an awkward position. For what I have experienced in the private sectors is that at least 80% of hiring managers (and male HR reps) try to take advantage of my case11 (!!). I've even had several hiring managers interviewing me with no intention of hiring me, shooting for "21" deal!! (they are referred as the Bactrian or bacterian? camel, I believe).

The President of Karlmon Dietech Information Technology tried to help me in when they had submitted my resume for the AFCPA Contract (and won), as the Director for this contract was reluctant (or afraid of being blamed, or getting cornered for bringing me in??). And as far as I know, the KDIT people got annoyed by that, so I backed out (340).

Also, the Head of ACIS Federal Communications Group tried to bring me into his group, but that didn't work out; Dr. Dube told me that he distributed my resume to his managers, but nobody had a right opening at that time (346).

I expected DSIA to be more firm on enforcing the EEO but the DSIA HR (recruiters) seems to be just the opposite. It appears to me that they are not being straightforward, try to confuse me and/or hoping for me to go away, passing me to another recruiter when I inquired about the positions that I had applied for or giving the status for the positions that do not reflect the actual status.

Ex: the position I applied for 5 months ago still shows "*Your application was referred to management for consideration. No selection has been made.*" And in one case, the status changed to "*Your application was referred to management for consideration, but someone else has been selected.*" right after I inquired the recruiter about the position.

I do feel that I had been given more chances than the average engineer, but that's also because I took chances looking for challenging tasks.

Again, I have no intention of causing you any trouble, all I am asking for is fair treatment. I have applied for the JOA 05-272 position just opened today (JOA attached).

Subject: EEO?

I have a lot on my mind, dealing with professional slump (or deadend?). A good news is that I may get appointed as a Senior Executive Services (SES) position for DSIA. The US Government has the *Equal Employment Opportunity (EEO)* policy, and my case will be a measure/enforcement of this policy. *SES is the highest ranking official of the US Government Agencies.

It will be highly political (and controversial) with me representing the (minority) single-woman professionals. Married women have already jumped up and down at the news that DSIA may grant me a SES, and I imagine that will become worse if/when I do become a SES; it will be a major BREAKTHROUGH.

I was trying to get a position as a GS-15 (highest rank for those who get hired by the Agency) but it wasn't going anywhere, and DSIA created a SES position. I am suspicious of the Black female responsible for the SES paperwork (her response to my email inquiry indicated that her intention was negative---), but I intend to follow the process and see . . .

To brag about myself,,, I am the #1 expert for the US DoD infrastructure (who is not working..). And many men are concerned with that; women are just jealous. Being on top of my field is not helping me get a job, it's more hurting me now, and that's why I am having such a TOUGH time; Less competent people are jumping up and down on my advancement in this field!!!!!!!!!!!!!!!!!!!

In the professional world, single women should do better since that's what they focus on, taking no time off for child birth, family care, etc., but those who are unreasonable always try to beat me with numbers (I am definitely out-numbered, needless to say).

My professional life has been like a roller-coaster riding. Many think I am the lucky one (and get jealous - *pain*). I suppose I have been pretty lucky, but my luck seems to be getting thinner as I gain more experience (and move up).

There is always someone (usually a jealous woman), who tries to rally people against me, and the double-minority (race and gender) like myself gets easily out-numbered. And it looks like the DSIA's "Hot Shot" babe is doing exactly that! If she is smart (or is a more mature professional), she would support me, as I will be setting the path for **** female professionals (those who men think are good looking and tend to give more chance).

Hopefully, this knucklehead babe will realize that she is only putting her foot into her mouth by doing that and calm down. Unfortunately, women usually are not as reasonable as men in most cases though, playing tiny and/or swayed by their emotions, based on my experience.

Anyway, it looks like DSIA is looking for my clone, which is good . . . Otherwise I will get all kinds of shooting by all kinds of people just for being a high-level female engineer!!!!!!!!!!!!! The only problem is that there may not be another woman engineer who has similar background as me . . .

Someone said that I was the "once in a lifetime catch!" It's flattering, but it's much easier being one of everyone.

The working world is still dominated by men, especially in the engineering field, and I get attacked everywhere, for one reason or another. Sometimes the pressure that comes with being in the male-dominated field is not easy to deal with . . . . The best I can do at this stage is to play along with DSIA, keep applying for new openings and hope for the best.

A winning attitude I learned is to be flexible and putting myself in the position of helping others, not demanding others to do things for me. It kinda sounds like JFK's inauguration speech, 'Ask not what your country can do for you, ask what you can do for your country.' Wow! How about that!? Must be a good one!

I contacted the DSIA DIRECTOR, *** Air Force General, and now it's up to the DSIA DIRECTOR to bring me into DSIA, regardless of what the rest of people may say or bitch about . . If not as a SES, maybe as a GS-15 or GS-14. There is not much salary difference, just a few thousands $$$/year; GS-15/3~4 gets higher salary than SES/1.

Here's what the DSIA DIRECTOR said (the last part of his e-mail) . . .

"DSIA is always looking for talented individuals and it's important that you continue to make yourself available and compete as these vacancies come open."   HDS

It looks like I may be joining DSIA as GS-14, under the Planning Dept. It's actually a fair level position (+/-) for my education/experience/talent, but some people are still trying to stop me (Monster, some says) from coming in, probably scared of me taking things over??? It's a wild card position, and it's up to me to develop the projects. Jerry thinks it sounds good, could be a bit much though, but there are not a whole lot of options. He is the most reasonable guy I know of, a single guy with good heart who knows this industry/people very well.

I do have a pending GS-15 position, and that is the right position for me, except that GS-15 is the "Supervisor" position (SES is more like the "Advisor" position). I am probably the best-qualified, but this position may be considered too much for an (Asian) female. It's too much for anyone right now, really, to lead the development of global information grid architecture, which is to establish the standardized baseline for the

DoD information systems. It's so huge that probably nobody really understands the big picture yet, I assume. Also, many men still seem to feel uncomfortable working under a woman, and it would be much worse working under an Asian woman, I imagine.

Most SESs are much older than me (in their mid 50's or 60's), I believe, but my case is a special case (1). I will probably get kicked out after one year if I get appointed as a SES, and I could kill the DSIA DIRECTOR as well; SES positions have one year of trial period. People are making an ISSUE out of my case (11), going against me getting appointed as a SES. I am not sure if I am ready to become a SES myself.

Between men trying to fit me into their personal needs and women picking on me for, it's hard to find a compromising position. On top of that, the HR says one thing, men say no, men ask for another, HR says no! I kept thinking about what my old Lockheed boss said to me, "It's too hard to work here!" That's exactly how I feel, so darn hard with people who are unreasonable and/or unwilling to compromise. Can't be 36, 355 is being too lucky, 51 is 8, 54 doesn't make sense (who's paying for . . . . how?!), forget 26!!!!!!!!!!!!!!!!

Anyway, I've done what I could, and now I will just have to wait to see what happens . . .

There is a famous saying about an engineer: 'The optimist sees the glass half-fill, the pessimist sees the glass half-empty, and the engineer sees the glass twice its size.' That's me, sharp and have tendency to over-analyze what I see, but I don't miss the point.

I have become the CENTER of the IT Industry politics, a crazy POWER POINT, the 'shrimp that gets crushed in the WHALES' fight?! Now the 1BOSS and people are fighting over me, it looks like, and I am trying to decide what to do about . . . ? I just got e-mails from his assistant (Lieutenant Colonel) and the HR Head, asking me not to communicate directly with the General (1BOSS).

I wonder if I should try to find another job, in case the DSIA job doesn't work out. I am under the impression that the DSIA DIRECTOR is getting cornered supporting me in . . . Jerry knows the DSIA DIRECTOR (he knows everyone in town, and out of town, actually) and says he is a good guy who will do the right thing. But there is not much he can do, if I get out-numbered. People who want to play with numbers will use the fact that I am an Asian-, and that will do.

Racial discrimination and harmony is the BIG CHALLENGE in America, and if you make a wrong statement about it, you would be a dead man before you know that you've opened your mouth wrong!!!!! I didn't even open my mouth, but someone created a racial situation around me once, and it was NOT good (I had to get out of the dead situation). It's really very deep rooted, and there is nothing I can do about. The best way to deal with it is to just ignore it. 'Not knowing is medicine' applies well in this case, I think. I emptied (and constantly try to empty) my head from anything related to racial discrimination, and that's the only thing I can do to help myself, really.

Over the years, I have become a better human-being, I believe, thanks to Ricky and other good quality people who I met. I changed my attitude towards others with 'good heart is better than smart brain' belief. I now look for those who have good hearts to keep around . . . Those with good hearts do not display the racial attitude. Those who are competent do not display the racial attitude (even though they may have some prejudice in their heart as we all do) if they think you are a good quality person.

Marriage is a different matter. Most high-quality White guys don't even consider marrying other race female, even if she possesses the best-quality. I would have married if I had found a right guy (interested in marrying me). It's better to be alone than being with a bad company (spouse), but being a single female seems to have a lot more limit (lower glass-ceiling) than the married women in the American IT industry (besides being an Asian).

It (married vs. single) is kind of a trade-off between security and freedom, I would say. And most people choose the security over freedom. There is an old saying, 'The best farming is the children farming.'

I thought about having a daughter at one point, but I didn't have the right guy to have a daughter with, obviously. So the thought had come and gone. For some reason, anyone who thought I might have a child thought that I would have a daughter (not a son).

It's been raining all day today, and I have been cooped up in the house all day, bored and feeling lonely . . . . Worried, too, about the DSIA job situation. I just thought about what the comedian Park Saang-Gyu said about the loneliness, "When you feel lonely, sleep!" Ha haa haaaa~~~

Subject: 6th Street Restaurant

I am pretty famous(?) in my neighborhood, which is mostly Blacks. I would say I am like an ugly duckling in this relatively poor neighborhood, probably one of the best-educated residents. I feel fairly comfortable though because I used to live here, 16-17 years ago, but otherwise, I would probably have never considered this area to find a home for myself. It's okay,, for temporary staying,,, well, I'd better fit myself in anyway since I have no other choice.

My next door is a White family (as White as Whites get, German-American), with two sons and two daughters all grown up. The youngest daughter still lives with them in their basement. It's pretty common for the oldest kid to live in the basement, as it is the largest space and is more private (more away from their parents' space). They have been living in this townhouse since when it was first built in 1970's.

My next-next door is a retired old White man who lives alone, Mr. White (his true last name). I say hi to him when I see him, but I don't know anything about him other than he puts a bag of peanuts under the tree behind <his-my next door-my house> every morning to feed birds and squirrels.

My next door neighbor guy is pretty friendly. He cuts my grass when he cuts his since I don't have a lawn-mower. This couple usually invites me to their church events, and they are very nice, polite and clean family.

There was a good mixture of Whites and Blacks before,, but now, it looks like there are a lot more Blacks than Whites in these townhouses. I bragged about how I turned this old house into a beautiful home, but Ricky did all the hard and big jobs, no need to say. I was just playing around mostly with cosmetic works (looks of the house).

People in this area seem to see me as an "ouster" of the white-color working world, for being too "outstanding" (and paying my dues like Martha Stuart). I heard someone saying, "She is "whiter than White."

Somehow people notice me everywhere,,, supermarkets, shopping malls, Home Depot, announcing my entrance with numbers, 317, 55, 461, 856, 1131, etc.

It surprised me that general people, even kids, in Pennsylvania, are aware of my case, and they seem so sure that it is me when they see me somehow. I don't wear noticeable clothes or put on much makeup. I don't even like clothes with strong/bright colors. When girls see me in boyish clothes, they said, "ah~aa~ it's the boy," like they have just discovered a secret. Most guys just look at me quietly, some with delighted smiles (they must think my look is just fine, I imagine).

Even my neighborhood restaurant has put up a new sign, "6th Street Restaurant" ^$^

I am flattered about the attentions and feeling pretty good about myself, despite my financial and job situation. I guess I am a born optimist, believing I would get what I deserve eventually. 'I will get to join DSIA with a reasonable position since I was a DSIA STAR**** who deserve the purple-heart medal,' I am thinking (hoping) . . . .

Subject: Men!

It seems that help is one-way street. Those who help you are always in the position to help you, and those who you have helped are never in the position to help you. The worst kind is those who you have helped turning around and becoming a backstabber, when they no longer need your help-. That's what I would call having a rotten "in-bok." (people luck).

Based on my experience, men are more logical and willing to compromise (reasonable, that is) than women, in general, in other word, more mature professionally.

Most men can't afford to have a mistress,,, so they look for someone to play with at work places; That doesn't cost them anything (the less cost, the better). Someone told me how men prefer to have a woman with huge butt as wife, more secure as other men wouldn't try to steal her from him (vs. having a child easier, as Korean older women would say). And men hate the other man getting a good looking babe (their stomach really hurts for that)..

Many married men and married women are all flirting around at work, if they can,, it's just that they pick on those who get favored by their boss. As a matter of fact, those married women who like to flirt with men are the ones who *jump up and down the hardest* on someone like me, a popular single. And it's usually a woman who likes her boss tries to rally people against me, if her boss shows me interest. Pretty hypocritical, I would say.

So, what's the solution? In the IT world, men hold most of the management positions, and some of them try to abuse their position when they see a good-looking woman ('Hokay, I gotcha!'). High or low, makes no difference. The only difference is that people make a lot of noise at the higher level!!!!!!!!!!!!!!!!!!!!!!!!

Here's my job situation with DSIA (11):

1) GS-14 Wild card position: This position has no specific responsibilities, basically to check everything operational in the DoD environment and plan/develop new tasks (Planning).
2) New GS-14 position (318) and another GS-14 position (319) under same group: These positions have specific responsibilities and it is the HR position, I believe (one is the back position and the other is the head position).

Now, I am trying to decide whether to apply for the new position(s) or not.. If I don't, the HR may use that as an excuse for not bringing me in . . . And if I do, the General may lose the ground for supporting the 1st position (back position). The HR (mostly women, except the Head) probably has no intention of bringing me in, but they need to at least pretend that they are trying the EEO (319). Most of the DSIA recruiters are females (except maybe there is one guy recruiter) and they have been trying to avoid me or find a reason to get rid of me ---.

What I have experienced with the private companies is that they try to kill my head, going for 54 deal (<u>salary cut down</u>). The wild card position is like between 54 and 39. I've offered all of the options, but they (management/HR) don't seem to agree with any of them,,, *just opposing an option without any better option*!!!!!!!!! There is no direction/rule, just different groups tossing my suggestion away . . .

I have feeling that the DSIA DIRECTOR may be in TOUGH position supporting ME (possibly supporting military Generals) . . . Majority of people are into making me a *tiny, unimportant* nobody-hole, no doubt (*relative superiority principle*, according to brilliant Chanstein). But I am who I am, and I am trying to make myself fit into the overall structure, being reasonable and flexible.

In any case, I am not going anywhere fast, for sure.

Subject: Background Investigation

Jerry is not cute (no Tom and Jerry there). As a matter of fact, he is one of the most aggressive guys, if not the most aggressive guy in the DoD IT field. Most people get intimidated by his fast fluent speech (including me).

OPM is investigating my background now, for my Top Secret Clearance. I was contacted by a Federal woman investigator this Monday, and she basically confirmed my address, my former bosses and references' whereabouts and their contact information. She said that they will arrange a face-to-face interview in Philadelphia area, where I am now.

Then on Tuesday, my DSIA friend told me that he was contacted by an OPM investigator working my clearance, and he sent me an e-mail stating . . .

"Today, I met with the OPM investigator working your clearance. I confirmed that you lived at Fairfax & Brookhaven . . . When I started answering questions about the work that you have done and where you have gone, it is pretty impressive."

It would be interesting to see where this investigation would take me, if I would get the SES seat after all (with the OPM clearance). In any case, I've informed the DSIA HR about the Federal Government working on my clearance, hoping that they would take the appropriate action.

I applied for two new GS-14 positions (318 and 319), but the recruiter is dragging her feet -- she probably hated that I applied for both positions -- I didn't give her an excuse not to forward at least one of the two to the hiring manager.

DSIA still hasn't selected anyone for the couple SES position or the GS-15 position supporting the GIG Architecture that I believe I would be the best candidate for. I bet I would be the best candidate for one of the couple SES positions as well, technicality-wise. My DSIA friend who reviewed my Technical Qualification Statement thought I would be the best candidate, too. But I would be lacking the management experience.

There are many older women working at large organizations in America, a lot more women and minorities at the Government (than private companies). The issue is the level and field.

The highest level for minorities in the Engineering field is GS-13 in most cases, as far as I know. It takes time to change the structure, and the attitude (*prejudice*) is the hardest one to overcome. I would have made GS-14 several years ago if I stayed with DSIA, but I left to expand my horizons, to become a better professional. I believe I have become a much more competent professional, but I seem to be paying for that instead of getting rewarded (-- instead of ++).

Jerry has been contacted by the DSS investigator. So, my clearance must be moving along . . .

Subject: No energy

I heard the news that the DSIA DIRECTOR has stepped down and new DIRECTOR is coming on board next week. Dunno what I am supposed to do??? I don't know if it has something to do with me or what? Should I send him some kind of note? I don't know what to say to him, speechless at this point, feeling dizzy,

. . . .

. . . .

Someone left an old newspaper on my door step. It's amazing how my neighbors know what's going on with DSIA & me even before I do. These Pennsylvanians are so keen, on top of the Washington DC. I wonder if that's because they are living in the land above the DC or what? People are sending all kinds of signals to broadcast what's going on with DSIA & me . . .

I learned that the General has been with DSIA for five years (he has fulfilled his five year tenure), but my DSIA friend led me to think that it had something to do with me (I am 1 there). I had a very good relationship with one of the DSIA Directors (a sector director) when I was with DSIA before, a smart and tough leader. There was a magic . . . . And with that magic, I had great experience! My heart was into my work. Thought I might have found a new magic, but I guess the timing wasn't right. I was so hopeful and so excited with the anticipation of a new magic . . . .

Now I gotta start again, and the bad part is that I am not going anywhere fast, not to mention that I am in low spirit to motivate myself. I am going to have to sit still for a while, keeping my courage and confidence, and keep hoping and believing that things (people) will be placed where it should be,,, eventually.

Apparently, the Black teenage girls pay close attention to what happens to me, looking at my case as their future. I often have some teenage girls hanging around in front of my house, trying to get a glimpse of me.

Officially, I am the first **11** case, and the Black teenage girls are trying to cheer me up, hoping that I will break up the minority-woman glass-ceiling, I imagine.

The word travels fast. Yesterday, there were 3-4 teenage girls and a little girl sitting in front of my next-door neighbor's house, and when I went out to get some stuffs from my car, I heard the little girl whispering to the others, "Is that the bitch?"

A cool female who lived in the same building where I was living in Fairfax exclaimed quietly when she first saw me, "That's a zet!" (high, speedy, and sexy, like a jet airplane). Thought that was an interesting word (she made it up instantly). Men often label females as a car, and many, especially young guys, think of their car as their baby. It would definitely be a lot easier to be a Sedan or even a Jeep . . . I like Jeep, that's a cool car . . .

Women seem to get tougher with the age, and men get weaker. Or is that men loosening and women trying to claim their sacrifice over the years?
I often run into those middle-aged women at the supermarket, who seemed to have tough expression embedded on their face (I can just see the sulkiness on their face). Could that be from putting up with her husband's bullshits? They usually give me a mean look, displaying their *sulkiness* one way or another (*gotta do that!*).

It's going to be a while for DSIA to settle my case, it looks like, and I am going to have to practice my patience . . . .

Subject: Lieutenant General Rey Era

I had been contacted and interviewed twice by an OPM investigator. He said that my brother-in-law should have my sister work for him, twice. I suppose that means the Federal Government is going to support work couples.

Some private companies have been supporting work couples, I know, mostly at the worker-level (but not at the management level or head-level). So, I expect things will be moving towards that direction, for the equality of man & woman. That's what everyone likes, really, to have someone close who they like and can trust.

Also, most people can use some breaks from the monogamy life-style. That gets pretty boring after a while, right? The couples stick together, more for the responsibilities for their kids than anything else, which can be pretty draggy, like having some rock on their shoulder. The higher one's socio-economic level, the drier (more uptight) it gets . . .

New Director, another 3-star Air Force General with "Jr" thing attached as part of his name, meaning they would be stuck-up, more or less (kidding), seemed like a shrewd guy (possibly not as straightforward as the old Director). I read his chronicle on DSIA website, and he just got promoted to take the DSIA Director responsibility.

My DSIA friend forwarded this new General's first e-mail to DSIA people, and it looked like he was implying **my case** and his intention about it, to bring me in with any position possibly less than SES. And I got the impression that he is less than thrilled to be the DISA Director-?

I contacted him to inform him of my job situation, and he opened some new positions. Now my job situation is . . . .

1) New SES position (HR): I will have to deal with a lot of pissed-off people, and I may be out after one year.

2) GS-14/15: it's the new position supporting the DIRECTOR (and his own military staff), enters as GS-14 and can move up to GS-15 with good performance, which will be perfect. The only problem is that I don't have any experience with any kind of Strategy work. I assume the retired high-ranking military officers will be good candidates for this type of work.

Which option do you think I should shoot for? Option #2 will be better, but I don't have the right experience.

Check http://www.afcea.org/signal/
***General in the picture is the new DSIA Director :).
Pretty good-looking, huh? He was the front page of another military IT magazine as well.

I was beginning to lose interest (hope) in DSIA because of their jealous recruiters and people playing with bullshits (even trying to use other's prejudice to play ganging-up's). Those who are secure about themselves are not jealous of others, but unfortunately, my status seems to make every women jealous. Anyway, I should stick around DSIA and see what happens since the new Director is good-looking (kidding) . . .

Speaking of recruiters (sigh),,,one recruiter had been promoted to GS-14 to bring me in, but instead, this stupid-overbearing recruiter kept me out, not processing my applications, even trying to tell me that she was the big shot there (and I am finished). It looked like she was even abusing her new senior position to boss other recruiters around, putting other recruiter's name as the contact person for the job applications she was responsible for (jobs that was created to bring me in), pissing the other recruiters off. I told her boss what she was doing, as I couldn't get clear answer from the other recruiters who seemed pretty disgusted by this arrogant recruiter (they wished me to tell their boss, actually).

Military people there are against the HR taking the 316 hat, but I need someone to process my application. She screwed it (and out)! This kind of crazy knucklehead female makes the situation really hard . . . .

Subject: Tough Situation

Now that the OPM issued me Top Secret clearance, it looks like some DSIA people want to kick me out of the country! I laughed when I heard about it last week (for the reason being I am too good). It is not going to be easy to join DSIA with the new Director, even with the HR Head's support. (*Some people seem to try to link me with the old Director's stepping down, even though his five year tenure was over),*

The DSIA Director opened up some other positions directly under him, and next day, the HR Director, I believe, opened up another position supporting Multi-National Information Sharing Systems, the project that I would be a better fit as the project name indicates. The HR Director is having this position open for **FIVE** days! (instead of 2 weeks).

It looks like both of them are trying hard to do the right thing, not talking to each other (conflicting each other). What am I supposed to do??? Now people are really annoyed by **ME!!!!!!!** I am trying to figure out how to resolve this situation; apply for the HR Director's new position (I will have his 5 authority in that case) or try to smooth the situation. How??? I am not in there, can't do much.

DSIA seems to have this Civilian/Military politics going . . . There are a lot more civilians than the military people there, who have been with DSIA for 20-30 years, whereas the military people are there as temporary members, for 2-3 years. Each service (Army, Navy, Air Force, etc) has representatives for various projects. And the General has his own military staff, working directly under him. The Military Generals are the link between <Military needs/funding> and <what DSIA does for the military, their customers>.

The Super-Star General has made another cover page for the magazine called the *Federal Computing Week* (Nov 7) with the title, "**DSIA Enters Rey Era**" (Rey is his last name): DSIA Enters in yellow on top of Rey Era in white, with the General standing with his arms crossed, looking worried.

I don't know what to think, I just have to believe that everyone will live for what his/her capacity and to keep my spirit high, believing in my-self. I feel bad for the General, having to deal with this situation. He must be under a lot of pressure.

The General has planned to have the Customer Conference in Las Vegas in May 1-4, right after the *Federal Computing Week* coverage. Someone hinted me that the General is in a tough situation, sending me a picture of Da Boss sitting at his desk alone, looking deadly serious with the door closed. Someone also hinted me that the General will be dispatched if he approves a GS-15 position that the HR is supporting.

It looks like the situation is deteriorating with the publication and the Las Vegas conference plan. Some people are shooting off very low-level 13 positions as a means to express their annoyance or opinion (to bring me/back down, possibly).

I guess that the best thing I can do is to just follow the rule. Those who should hire me keep *shooting off other positions after I applied for the position opened/well-qualified.*

I am checking the possibility of joining the United Nations, but there are not many job openings for general public (and the term may be limited to 2 years). It won't hurt to check and apply for the positions that match my experience there in any case.

Subject: Ideal vs. Reality

The DSIA DIRECTOR & ME seem to be the WATCH of the DoD IT industries these days (talk of the town, entertainment, monkeys, "Micky & Mini" Mouse).

I suppose the power is the dirty game, but with everyone trying to exercise even a little tiny power they have, whether it is from their position, money, or whatever,,, it gets ridiculous. What can I (or anyone in control) do about? The difference is the degree and the manners, and I can only hope that I wouldn't have to deal with the dirtiest and the tiniest (those who play hassle when they don't have any justification or don't have anything to pick on, using others' jealousy or prejudice).

It's not just married or jealous women playing with their emotions, but guys are playing dirty, too, like that big guy you met, who tries hard to get me, with "keep her down/small" attitude! When they can't (get rejected), they turn around and try to gang people against ME!! Those lower-level (or rejected) guys' *sim-tong* is just as bad, if not worse.

Some guys try to pick on anything and everything just like jealous females do. It was guys who try to threaten me with "TOP OUT!" for the Technical Director position, etc.

I see why the OPM Investigator recommended work couple. That's the best possible option except too many people are hindering it . .

People are basically self-centered (with varying degrees), and they interpret or twist things in a way to satisfy their ego. It's also a matter of intention. Those with good intention see the good part of the situation, and those with bad intention see (or look for) the reason to go against, no matter what. The world is full of crap, picking and attacking, all trying to make themselves feel better, in a way.

I applied for the GS-14/15 IT Strategy position, and the next day, DSIA opened up a few other positions under the DIRECTOR, with another IT Strategy position working at the Pentagon. I also applied for the new position supported by the HR Director (5), then gave them my preference.

Power over Justice? More like Reality over Ideal (or rule), I would guess. If I went with the HR Director, I could have just killed him, I was afraid. But if I didn't apply for his position, he would have looked silly or it could be used as an excuse why DSIA can't bring me in.

People (my neighbors) are making a lot of noises!!!!! It must be going pretty ROUGH there *^%()$%#@!

The General made the cover page of another Air Force magazine last month. I was under the impression that he didn't have a good start with DSIA for what happened with his predecessor & ME . . . In any case, I wouldn't be surprised if he becomes the Chairman of the Joint Chief of Staff (****), or even the Secretary of Defense in the future. The Defense Secretary Rumsfeld is a former Air Force and the current Chairman of the Joint Chief of Staff is Air Force, as well.

One of the former DSIA DIRECTOR (*** Air Force) is the President of the largest IT company called SDE, the SDE Federal Systems Sector. He was the first Black General to serve as the DSIA DIRECTOR,,, and SDE has become much more open to minorities for higher positions (some former DSIA people moved to SDE, too). I had an interview with SDE a few years ago, and there was an Indian guy ("In-Do") holding the most advanced technical position.

My philosophy is to 'know yourself' first - I think Socrates was one of the greatest philosophers just for that wisdom alone. I would add keep your feet on the ground and adjust yourself to reality. Those who adapt and compromise with reality are the ones who prosper (or survive, at least).

I know a relatively cool woman HR at the small company where I worked as the program manager and she said, about men, "They will do anything!" (! = fxxx). That's their bottom line (motivation). I get motivated to work harder when I am attracted to a man who I work with, to impress him, I guess :).

Subject: Turbulence

I have some difficulty keeping my spirit high these days, too much disappointment with my job situation. It's probably no-win situation for me (I am not supposed to win here), but I don't have other option.

The HR Director is doing everything he can to help me in. He supported me as his work couple, but that went nowhere (of course not). Now he is wearing the FIREHAT trying to bring me in as a GS-15, trying to enforce the Equal Employment Opportunity rule (+++). He is trying to tell people that he will fire those who don't follow the rule is what I can figure going on there . . . . I imagine that the recruiters are afraid of handling (*mishandling*) my application.

I am trying to stay cool, but it's NO FUN being alone in this cold world surrounded by strangers who seem to be all out to get me. It's better (definitely easier) to be one of many, sharing same interest, life-style, etc.

My choice for joining DSIA now is either as GS-15 (HR Director's call) or GS-13 (illegal back position). What's wrong with GS-14, which is a reasonable level? They (recruiters/moms-) ruled it out with the reason that it will make me too big(10) or that's being too lucky. A cheap tact in an attempt to bring me down to GS-13 (figuring that men wouldn't support GS-15 position), no doubt..

What do you think will win? Justice or Reality? I am sticking with Justice, win or lose. At least I will be protected by law, be able to justify myself (vs. get killed by bullshit, one way or another).

My application for a GS-15 position is supposed to be submitted to the selecting manager, with the HR Director's support, but it will probably go nowhere. Being a boss doesn't mean much in my situation. Nobody follows the rule or direction, if not try to corner the boss for supporting ME . . Boss may make more money, but these people have no respect (if not hate) their boss. For my case, it's just so easy to gang-up against ("yellow"). And for a boss' babe, they will shoot both to death!!!!!!!!!!!!!!!!!!!!!

Anyway, it looks like DSIA is going through some turmoil (lots of change) . . . . One of their well known Engineer, Director of DSIA Network Operations, Joe, who was a candidate for the first couple SES with me, left DSIA -- My guess is that the *couple SES positions* were created with negative intention.

Another guy who took Joe's old position (and just got appointed as a SES) is leaving DSIA, too. And the #1 woman SES there got pulled out to be in the team working for an Undersecretary of Defense (Mr. Rumsfeld's Technical Staff). She is a HUGE BITCH according to Jerry (he didn't actually say that, but he had hinted me to stay away from her).

My DSIA friend told me that they are going through reorganization, and it's going to take a while for them to settle the situation with new boss.

I've been doing some research on satellite stuffs, and Gosh, this is what advanced technology is all about. Rocket science it is! I am not trying to learn how the satellite is designed (even attempting to learn that would be ridiculous), just how the satellite is used for data communications.

I had applied for a position with UN, and it looks like they may be interested in bringing me in for another position (or maybe the other way around, no way in). They just opened a new position, P-5 (equivalent to GS-14/15) as the Chief Communications Engineer, for 15 days, which is very unusual.

The UN usually have any positions open for a long time, a month or longer, and sometimes for several months or even indefinitely (=> until they find the right person). I imagine people who work for UN are pretty special (unusual) people, and some of the positions sound like it will be very hard to find the right candidate just for the technical qualification requirements.

I went to the Korean supermarket, Assi, today, and I was thinking how my life does not have the last defense (or security). Family is the last defense, who will be there for you if/when something happens to you,,, and for me, there is no one who will be there for me => I can't afford to make a mistake (ex: have a car accident and get hurt) or even get sick. The thought of that made me a little nervous driving today.

Someone said, about me, "She has been driving 75 miles an hour." I don't know if that's the case. What I do know is that having someone who you can depend on (like your spouse or some family member) is what every-one needs (security). There is a famous, all-time-favorite, American cartoon, called Charlie Brown,,, and in that cartoon, a young boy is always dragging a blanket with him (referred as the "security blanket").

I had a dream of Dad last night again, and he was holding (covering) my hands with his while I was sleeping. My hands were outside of the blanket, cold, and he was warming my hands with his. I guess I keep dreaming of Dad because he was the warmest person who I know/remember (and I feel so cold, these days). Dreams reflect the state of one's mind, and I must be fearing that everyone is out to corner me, subconsciously.

A song just popped into my head . . *Sweet dreams are made of years, ~~~ I traveled the world and seven seas, and everybody is looking for something ~ Some of them want to use you~ some of them want to be used by you ~~ Someone of them want to abuse you~ someone of them want to be abused ~~~~*

Use or abuse, that's what life seems to be all about . . . ? We all need to be used (useful), and hopefully in a good way, the way that you deserve and makes you feel good about yourself.

I passed the e-mail that I received from the old Director to the new Director, and apparently, the new General gave the direction to bring me in up to GS-15 (SES-) since a bunch of new positions opened up.

Men (or everyone) are against me joining as GS-15, and the recruiters (or maybe all women) hate the idea of me being "13." They are like 'forget 13-, we will support 49.' Men are just the opposite, of course, they are singing high to bring me in with the back position.

Now it looks like some DSIA people are trying to make an issue out of my color openly, as a means to bring me down, announcing a new opening at an off-site location in "Indian Head," Maryland. It's a famous Joint Test Lab, actually, but I doubt that they have any intention of bringing me in (49).

Whatever their intention may be,,, there are two ways to look at this as far as I am concerned: 1) it can be a good ground work to move up, 2) they bring me in to tell the General that I am in, and then quietly get rid of me when it gets quiet.

I have attracted too much attention, and they have to do something to quiet things down (or to pretend to follow the General's direction, at least). I really don't know what to think . . I've seen too many negative intentions lately. People are playing with bad tactics everywhere.

I may be too clean (too uptight or too righteous), and I need to learn to play the dirty game, to be successful, even just to survive . . . I applied for the GS-13 position working at the test lab in the Indian Head, and I told the HR Director that I did. Otherwise the recruiter wouldn't process my application, I am pretty sure. And crazy it is, my neighbors knew about <me and this Indian-Head position> that afternoon, and they were sending all kinds of signals.

The HR Director is really the biggest supporter of me, and some people have been trying to tell me that I am being very lucky for that. But some guys hate the idea that I am communicating with him as they wouldn't be able to play their bullshit on me!

The Head guys have good reasons why (or how) they have become the Head. They are born (or learned) to be RESPONSIBLE ('Responsibility is what makes one great').

My boss at Lockheed Martin (one of the most experienced managers of all, who retired from IBM) told me that a few were born to lead (and most were born to be the followers). I am born to be a boss (so I have been told anyway),,, but that just doesn't work, being an Asian woman engineer in America; born in the wrong place at the wrong time, maybe, as someone told me. All I get to accomplish is getting tougher, with nothing to show for . . . .

Anyway, the Air Force guys are supporting me more openly and actively now including (implying) my status with DSIA in their regular email broadcasting . . . .

Here's new development for my job situation with DSIA:

- GS-13 position working at the Test Lab in Maryland.
- GS-15 position as Telecommunications Manager, supporting Joint Chief of Staff (JCS); The Head of JCS is ****Air Force General, at the present time.

DSIA managers are shooting off new GS-14 positions again. Many are against me getting the position supporting the JCS, I figure, but they can't afford to go against the JCS! That's where the big money is coming from, the POWER HOUSE! It is the right position for me, but it is a scary or annoying position for everyone, probably.

The lower-level DSIA people have been trying to tell me that they are going to *fax me out* (gang-up against me), if I join DSIA above the GS-13 position,,, trying to bring me in as GS-13 to have some fun,,, And the recruiters are trying to take the 13 status off of me at the door!

I was actually reluctant to apply for the Telecommunications Manager position, figuring how people would resist, but the DSIA extended the deadline, so I had to apply whether it is waste of my hope or not. I may be the right & only candidate who can fill this position, but still, it's almost too special ... Jerry tried to suggest a position like this, supporting the Generals, some time ago, then he backed out. The Generals may appreciate, but others would have trouble dealing with a baby with Generals on her back!!!!!!!!!! Jerry has been known this new DSIA DIRECTOR and thought that this General & I would be a good match!

People are still arguing about mumbo-jumbo's; 26 vs. 36, "12" (GS-13) vs."13" (GS-13 or GS-14), Military vs. Civilian, Internal vs. External (Customer Support - foot shooter), etc., etc.

I tend to clarify everything in black and white, and I am learning that some things are better left as grey . . . I watched the Korean TV drama "Jaang-Heu-Bin," and one thing I learned from that drama is what Kang Boo Jaa (Dae-Bi) said to Jaang-Heu-Bin when she first entered the palace, *"You need to learn the wisdom to pretend that you don't know, instead of trying to show off how bright you are!"*

There is no ideal situation, but I can't stand how some people are trying to tie me down to a going-nowhere position. Everyone has some *prejudice*, but there is difference in the degree and how they handle it. If a GS-13 position is what I can join as, that's a start (reality). I am just holding off from the *going-nowhere back-* that some people are trying to establish, abusing my 11 status!!!

It's a wonderful (and crazy) world, and there are so much to explore. Price for everything though. I chose to explore the other possibility, paying the price of being lonely for the challenge, freedom and excitement. My strength and confidence are two of my biggest assets, I believe, personality and wits are next. Look is plus+++++.

These day, some men seem to consider my strength and confidence as negative assets though (those who prefer to abuse a woman). I need to develop one more filter to filter those out!

Subject: Status of Open/Pending Positions

LTG Rey:

It's much easier to join an organization without being noticed, I guess, but I seemed to have made a lot of noise in the process of trying to join DSIA again and don't seem to have that choice.

I am under the impression that the Air Force is concerned with my whereabout,,, and here is the update of where I am with DSIA. It seems that DSIA people are now making an endless make-no-sense (in my opinion) issues incl AUTHORIZED = NOT AUTHORIZED????? I have trouble figuring out how that works!!!!!

Listed is just the half of the positions that I applied since your "era"? Some recruitments got cancelled,,, and others, I am not sure if there were any intention of hiring anyone in the first place!

< List omitted . . . .>

In case some people are making an issue out of my life style,,, Secretary Rice is a single woman, probably a lot more dedicated to work than married women with 4-5 children, I would think. 7=7 (7->5).

I attended the GIG-BE Industry Day a few years ago, and one of the PMs (Lt Col somebody, forgot his name) said, "**Chickens get involved, DSIA commits.**" Thought that was pretty cool and I actually wrote that down on my notebook.

Subject: Choice

Yakking is good. I feel less lonely talking to you and also feel relieved of the stressful situation, letting my frustration out on you. Sometimes I write to you but don't send it, and that still relieves the stress.

I don't look like a model, I look like a well educated intellect; minimum makeup, no jewelry (just earrings), simple clothes. I don't even like clothes with female colors (red, pink, etc.) and prefer blue, green, and neutral/brownish color clothes. I have no interest in being someone's 26 personally. In my dictionary, 26 or 36 is for work.

American guys are pretty cheap, as far as I know, possibly because the type of guys who I have met are eggish -or- maybe they are just used to financially independent women and prefer that way. They shoot for minimum expense & maximum sex! Real cheapies, in a way.

I am confused about the situation with DSIA, whether to apply for another position or just let it be with the positions that I have already applied. The GS-15 Telecommunications Manager position supporting the Joint Chief of Staff (this position is like "Bull's Eye") seemed to have generated more tension between DSIA DIRECTOR (& Military Generals) vs. People. I don't know what to do, apply for another position and let the General "off the hook" or ??? If he doesn't bring me in, he would look bad, but people just don't like the idea of "him" trying to bring me in . . .

There is an old friend of mine working as a contractor supporting the General, but because he is a contractor, he has little control over helping me in . . . Not much I can do from outside other than keep applying for new openings. It seems like they have fun with my one-way e-mails, open more positions every time I shoot an e-mail to them, circling around and around . . .

The best thing I can do is to be myself, do the right thing and see what happens, let it be . . . . Things get screwed when you try to control too hard. In fact, it doesn't make much difference whether I try to control the situation or not. America is full of those *control freaks* screwing things up, with no intention of changing their attitude regardless of what I say.

We all make our own choices that we have to live by. You chose a man for love and family, and I chose an opportunity for myself. Some women have it all, love and family and career, and smart enough to prioritize her life to be in order and be happy. I am not that fortunate, I guess.

Most women I know seem to have some difficulty with their marriages, either unhappy or bored. Some are just putting up with their husband's crap for the sake of their children (otherwise she would consider divorcing him). I got divorced because I needed more excitement. Most women are pretty busy when kids are young, but when they reach the middle-age with kids all grown-up, not even living with them, they feel empty, right?

It goes both ways, both men and wives . . . Middle-age people need more excitement, not necessarily getting divorced . . .

It's not a bad idea to have a role model and try to imitate the role model. Not all from one specific role model, possibly from several; this way from one model, that way from another, etc.

Who is my ideal image of women, I wondered . . . ?

I like smart and strong woman who pioneers her destiny, beyond the conventional limit. Hillary Clinton, I guess, would be closest to my ideal image of women. Actually, there is something that Hillary Clinton and I have in common -- There are a lot of men who want to kick her out of this country, and there are a lot of women who want to kick me out of this country! Someone actually told me to "*Take Hillary to Korea with you and have her run for the Presidency over there!*" *@#$%^&***

Cheers to our choice!

Subject: Born to be . . . ?

We are having some beautiful Spring days, nice and sunny, perfect temperature, even with warm breeze~~~ I took a little ride out, with my convertible top open -- it's the only thing that makes me feel okay these days.

I am trying to determine what I am born to do may be . . . Americans use the word *dog* for a lot of things (they definitely like doggies). Bosses are referred as the Big Dog, Jerry refers himself as a wild hunting dog, there are little dog . . . I guess I am an under-dog, although some people seem to refer me as the hotdog!!!

It's still like a whirlpool ("ssang-naan-ri") with DSIA. One position that I applied (GS-15) under another Directorate got *cancelled,* and I may be the only one who can fill the Telecommunications Manager position since

DSIA opened it as a back position supporting the Joint Chiefs of Staff. But I had the General off the hook, applying for other new positions, so there will be no "Marching On . . . " I checked the Joint Chiefs of Staff members, and Oh My God, these Generals all look "moo-seo-weo"!!!! One of them has no hair (no relation to Yul Brynner there).

I can't think of anyone who may be qualified and brave enough to do that, except Lori, but she is already GS-15 working at the Pentagon. So that's hard to dispute against, but apparently people are arguing about me getting this position. The Financial Group seems to be supporting this position (need money to run the place, I suppose).

This GIG Operations Directorate is *shooting off* all kinds of positions, probably trying to steer me away from this Telecommunications Manager position. The Principal Director, Vice Principal Director, and the Deputy Principal Director, "TOGETHER",,, they opened a GS-13 position, as their Assistant!?#$%#.. And one of the Division Chiefs under this Directorate opened a GS-13/14 position, etc. etc. (smoking the right position out)!

I am just trying to stay cool, not saying anything, let them *mumbo-jumbo* all they want! I am not worried about what others may be thinking or would treat me (tough!). I just want a reasonable job that I can do a good work, be useful, and pay my bills.

I watched the DSIA Industry Day video, and the General was very polite, rather soft-spoken, not like the tough Generals who you would imagine. He is even somewhat "baang-jeong"(light) putting his hand to his fore-head to check the lights and making some quick moves. And OMG, the

HR Director looks like a hard-core, pretty "SSAAL-BEOL" with very short hair (kinda makes me think of German Mafia, with light blonde hair, not the Caecilian Mafia)!

The Lockheed Martin HR Director looked like a movie star and looked very compassionate, and that was my idea of the HR Head, rather soft and compassionate. I guess I'd better not assume things. The DISA HR Head looks like he would just PUNCH people around!!!

My guess is that there will be more people against--- for the position supporting the Joint Chief of Staffs . . . Maybe the best thing to do is to walk away from DSIA and get a job at someplace else, start something new, if possible? I still may have the possibility of joining the UN, but I don't know if and when???

It's imperfect world, one way or another. Even getting a spouse is a package deal. People are full of it ("sim-tong"), and you see more of the dissatisfied or uncompromising side of people as you get older and smarter. Maybe that's why there is an expression, *"grumpy old man and cranky old woman."*

What I appreciate most about myself these days is my sense of humor. Without it, I'd be pretty darn depressed now. You have no idea how much I get attacked by others and how hard others try to shake me down!! Nerve of steel, some people said about me, and sense of humor, that's how I hang on, in this crazy rat-race environment!

These days, I am like a 'WALKING STATEMENT', and I have to be careful of what I wear. I do wear the American designer clothes with logo sometimes, like Tommy Hilfiger sportswear with **tommy** written on the front (to actually make a statement). People scrutinize me (trying to find something to pick on, more or less) and make noises. I don't need bad noises, and my guess is that wearing expensive European designer clothes will generate bad noise. I still do what I want to do and wear what I want to wear, but I try to look more "low-profile" (nothing gained annoying people).

In the movie, *Silence of Lamb*, Anthony Hopkins tells Jodie Foster (FBI agent) how one can tell a person's class, by their shoes. Since that movie, people seem to start looking at other's shoes more, if they want to figure the person out, or to make a judgment; I had some people looking at my shoes, of course. Ha ha~

My Toyota convertible is silver/platinum color with black top (the opening part). Others say that the car fits my image very well. In America, silver is the most preferred car color, it's high-tech looking and the most durable (least color fading). Toyota is known for sturdiness; Toyota cars never break down, solid. So middle-age, practical people like Toyota.

Someone said that the winning formula in this world is to have the snake's smart (ability to make others do what you want) and pigeon's purity (good intention). Sounds about right, isn't it?

A well-known Japanese real-estate broker and writer, Robert Kiyoski, says that success is finding the genius in oneself. Robert Kiyoski was a real estate broker, and he wrote a book when he was 50 years old, <*Rich*

Dad, Poor Dad: What the Rich Teach Their Kids About Money--That the Poor and Middle Class Do Not!>, that has been one of the best sellers for 5 years and made him famous.

I don't know what the genius in me is, still trying to figure out what that may be . . . ? I picked the right field, Engineering (based on my IQ, I guess), but I don't think I am all that great. I can do the work, but I haven't invented anything, so . . .

Lately, I have slown down, intentionally (more like I had no choice but to slow down). I am like getting punished for being too smart (instead of getting rewarded), dealing with **15** (the best-qualified out). Things have turned upside down for me; merits -> faults, forward -> backward (-> forward???, that's the question). My head is "dd~i~n~g~", dealing with everyone's attitude change!

I am getting old, and all this wasted time (time of standing still) is killing me. I could be doing a great work and keep some men very happy. What a waste of talent! People tell me that I have a lot of energy . . . . And men tell me that I am the energy for them . . . .

What am I supposed to do . . . . ?

Is the spring rain supposed to be romantic? I am feeling rather down this morning, with gray sky and rain, thinking about my going-nowhere situation here . . . Love is the most powerful thing, but I gave up on love. Like Tae Jin-Aa's song, *Ssaa-raang is not for everyone?!*

I was obsessed with a Lockheed Martin Vice President (President now) and learned that he was pretty racial (OUCH!, that really HURT, d-e-e-p-down!). He made me appreciate Ricky and made me see what I had done to Ricky. How I was not nice to him, thinking nothing of abusing and shattering down his emotions (thinking I was too good for him).. I learned my boomerang lesson; 'What goes around, comes around' . . .

Just read about a British guy who is walking around the world. Can you imagine doing that? He intended to walk from the tip of South America to his home (England), and he has been walking for seven years. Caught in Russia for not obtaining the entrance-stamp and may get kicked out. He is half-way through what he set out to do.

How about Martha Stewart's new adventure? She is the home decorating doyenne and owns the Company called Omnimedia that manufactures household decorating goods (curtains, towels, trash cans, paints, etc., etc.). Like that wasn't enough, she has jumped into building homes now, inspired by her own homes; she has multiple homes at different locations. She is in her 60's and still looks good, going strong, stinking RICH and wants to get RICHER. Money makes money.

All kinds of people make up this world, and that's what makes the world interesting. Could you imagine how boring it would be if everyone follows the same path their parents had taken, have the same life style of getting married and have children?

I inquired about the Telecommunications Manager Position, and GEEZ, every group opened new positions the following day! Still the same *argument,* basically; men (management) are willing to settle with GS-14, and HR/moms seem to insist on GS-13/GS-15! Dunno what will get accomplished by this endless shooting off of new positions . . . ?

Pointing out problems in the beginning is okay, but some people just keep pointing out a problem, offering no solution. Who needs that!? That's no help, just annoying!! Anyway, I am beyond the frustration, just trying to stay cool (calm), keeping my mind off,,, doing the gardening and painting my fence (and my neighbors' fences).

Maybe I could drop down and work at an off-site location, but it's usually worse when I try to bring myself down. Nevertheless, I always keep the 'one-step back for two-step advance' strategy. The problem is that there are more people who try to push you two-step back (and use that as an excuse to keep you there) when you are willing to take one step back.

As far as I could tell, the DSIA Executives are screaming to stop the married women from volunteering to be a back to them (26); Moms are very aggressive, more aggressive than men, in some ways. Most men are not interested in the work couple (they may be interested in a tiny, cute 52!).

Jerry told me that he sees some good-looking Asian women at work,,, and he says "hi" to them, but they wouldn't say "hi" back to him avoiding the eye contact. That made me laugh; those women must be smarter than me! He also told me about how some companies would hire the Business Development people, strip off the contact information, and fire them. Sounded like he was telling to be careful not to let someone strip off my hat!

Too damn much politics and the abuse of democratic principle (# game, that is), for sure. All I see these days is bad tactics, and the best I can do is to play dumb - I've decided not to struggle too hard. *Just play along and see what happens* . . .

Nice guy finishes last in the working world, I read somewhere. Some Asian guys say it's them who finish last in the American working world. There are a few who do well, and a good/technical PhD degree is a must in that case with good communication skills.

Anyway, I've applied for a position with Booz Allen Hamilton, working in Korea (Kun-Saan) as the "host country liaison." It's not really my line of work, so I don't have much hope. If they don't have a better candidate, I may be considered. No harm done. I applied to see what happens and I did submit a good cover letter, mentioning that I attended the Yon-Sei university (one of the three "Sky Universities" in Korea). Keeping my fingers crossed (=> wishing for luck).

Subject: W~e~e~i~n~g

GEEZ, about 15-20 Emergency Vehicles (fire trucks, ambulances, etc.) have just passed by my house, w~e~e~i~n~g w~e~e~i~n~g w~e~e~i~n~g

These people just wouldn't leave me alone, you know? They say that I am the best ever! Even the best of the best! Being the best is good, but I am not sure if this is a good one to be the best at . . . . ? It may be a doomed best. Like the old saying, *'there is nothing to eat at the famous party!'*

Still the same situation with DSIA. All of the positions have been closed (got cancelled or some other candidates got selected), and the only one left is the Telecommunications Manager position supporting the Joint Chiefs of Staff as the Director's backup. DSIA can't afford to make a wrong move for this one, and I imagine that the General is pressured but reluctant (can't afford) to bring me in for this position.

They are still trying to bring me in,, as GS-13,,, keep making up new positions for me, and I guess I should be thankful. What I can determine is that they have conflicts with every group trying to pull me in different directions, NOT willing to compromise: Military, HR, Married women, Blacks, White females (recruiters), White males, Management.

It's IMPOSSIBLE with every group insisting on their ways only. I don't believe that the DSIA recruiters are posting the job status correctly - I am suspecting that some of them are making up the *b.s.* status, doing nothing with my applications.

There's a new movie, <Devil wears Prada>, with Meryl Streep in. I don't own any Prada things, don't wear anything fancy. I can just imagine how people will jump up and down on me, if I did. Maybe there are other Devils, Wallstreet Devil or whoever I don't know about,,, and they are doing just fine, but not me, the Military Devil.

One of my old boss at DSIA advised me *not to think that everyone was out to get me;* I must have appeared to be very protective of myself (or insecure). I didn't know this country better then, so that was a good advice then. Now, I know this country better, and I do think that everyone is out to get me!!!!! Maybe not everyone, but many people are OUT TO GET ME, I know.

It's very hard for different races to become real friends. Even people who came from different backgrounds (same race in the same country) don't become good friends, in most cases, having different points of view to begin with (=>no common ground, no bonding). I have not seen any good Black/White friends in America, if they don't hate each other. How long have they lived in the same land together? What I see is the deep (unspoken) hatred.

The challenge is how I can overcome the resistance of home-towners having been selected for a special position for the first time?????

Subject: 06-DEU-900/06-797KT/06-846KT

Mr. Manning:

The listed are the last six positions that I applied, and some of the positions seem to be up in the air (not being processed) as shown on the Resumix . . . DSIA recruiters may need your (or hiring manager's) specific direction to process my application for these positions . . . ?

<list omitted . . .>

Apparently, different groups have different/un-agreeable interests, and it's going nowhere (and I am the one who gets blamed for and is paying for, for everyone's *somebody do something'* attitude). **WHO IS SOMEBODY DOING IT? HELLO!**

OPM had issued me Top Secret clearance in Sep 05, and how many positions have I applied with DSIA since? Pardon me for saying this, but I would have to say that DSIA is pretty dysfunctional (or maybe it's me who is pretty confused?)!

I don't see the sense of keep applying for new openings/!@#$%^&*

It's been dragging on far too long,,,,, just going around the endless loop; can=can't, in=out, authorized=not authorized, etc. (sounds like "Mission Impossible")?

LTG Rey and everyone:

It looks like DSIA/DoD Community has a lot of new openings?!?

My recommendation is to bring me in with 06-846KT (GS-13 position under IA/NetOPs Group); This position seems like the most reasonable (agreeable) position. It will be impossible for one person to satisfy and be acceptable to everyone (one person->one group). **LTG Rey and Mr. Montemarano's approval to bring me in . . .**

The OPM's recommendation for me was the work couple, but apparently, that would be hard to realize at this stage,,,, and I would like to suggest "one step at a time!" If DSIA wishes to continue this DEVIL thing, I will select the appropriate and talented individual to carry that on (trying to take the HAT off at the door is BAD,,, it is not meant to be carried on that way!).

I am doing the best I can to help resolve this situation. I personally think that GS-13 level is pretty unfair; I was GS-13 in 1993.

Hope this helps the DSIA/DoD Community!

CVQ is not only hijacking my e-mails, but they also seems to be hijacking e-mails of those who I send e-mails to (maybe not everyone, just a few selected ones), and they seem to distribute the hi-jacked e-mails to their vendors/customers, as far as I could tell. One of their show hosts actually mentioned them doing "selective listening" . . .

One obvious reason is to increase the sales, as their customers seem to indicate interest in me (and those around me), and the other reason is pretty *RIDICULOUS* (almost looks like they are trying to prove that they are bigger/stronger than the Military/DSIA.

That's a CRIME to hijack others' e-mails, isn't it?

Could you PLEASE check with the security people (NSA or whoever) if there is a way of catching them and stop them from doing that (by monitoring their activities or whatever)? If CVQ cleans this hijacking activity before the security people get to them, some of their vendors will be able to verify that, I imagine; Some of their conscientious vendors were trying to tell CVQ to be more considerate of others – those who get their emails hijacked and abused-.

I wanted to let you know as soon as possible. It's possible that CVQ captured your work e-mail address from the last e-mail that I sent to you; I heard one of their hosts playing someone's voice, saying to their viewers, "Ladies, we got the jackpot!" It sounded like your voice. They babble about my DSIA friend as well, referring him as the master of footwork who is dancing with the star (me). And Dan as the light. They must have hijacked my temporary yahoo e-mail address, too, that I used to write an e-mail to Dan asking him about the e-mail hijacking/fix, about a week ago or so.

It looks like an air-cheap crook's "quality control" (screwing)of military IT environment, with little knowledge of the ground on top of the ridiculous air-blown ego.

Subject: 07-274KP (215)

LTG Rey:

Could you **authorize** the position 07-274KP (GS-855/1550-15) under GES/GE21-Integration Engineering Division for my case (15)? I am 15 for the GES Directorate's GIG tasks just based on my GCCS experience.

I believe it's a fair position for my background and qualification. It's not one of the more demanding or visible positions, just a good position to contribute my GCCS and other related experience as the reviewer.

To be fair, DSIA should pay me for the time consumed (Sep. 05 - Feb. 07) due to *ganging-up's.* I've tried to join DSIA a lot more than enough, having been PATIENT, as you know (with many headaches along the way, probably, just as I've had MANY headaches myself).

It's just too darn hard with different groups ganging up against 1-, 2-, 3-, 4-, 5-, 6-, . . ., **13-.**

Subject: DSIA is WIDE-OPEN to CVQ and its viewers

I am under the impression that CVQ is hijacking some of the DSIA personnel's e-mails & distribute to their customers (as a way of attracting their customers' interest/curiosity).

CVQ has been hi-jacking my e-mails (to increase sales, as their customers show interest in ME) and those who I send e-mails to, and now it sounds like they are hijacking DSIA Senior Management's e-mails (Mr. Manning, LTG Rey, and possibly some others); CVQ definitely has some piece of DSIA picture (HQ/HR) and talks about what happens at the DSIA in their shows, vaguely and possibly twisted . . . .

I may be wrong (or over-analyzing/reacting to what I hear), but according to the CVQ people's mumbo-jumbo's, it sounded like Dan was unhappy with DSIA not bringing me in & LTG Rey was upset about Dan not supporting his GIG work anymore and had issued red status for me . . . ??? They are mentioning that I am getting "knocked out" at the door, too.

Some of the CVQ hosts/vendors actually tried to communicate to me through the camera (looking at the camera). Now, it looks like I am like the CVQ/their customers' Global Positioning System for women. I guess those exceptional single women, such as the Secretary Rice and Oprah Winfrey, don't count, not to mention many women SES's at DSIA and other organizations. They are soooo interested in me, to my surprise,,, pursuing the back and/or the **work couple** idea.

I had asked Jerry Hanson, my old Lockheed colleague (my friend/advisor), to look into this, as I was under the impression that CVQ was hijacking his e-mails, about a week ago or so.

Apparently, DSIA is still trying to bring me in or disputing with my case,,,, and I thought I should inform you that CVQ is watching DSIA (and my case) and making a big noise that I don't need (or DSIA doesn't need, I am sure).

I am very frustrated of less competent people trying to ride on me (thinking that it's okay to do that because I am an asian, playing with #s), CVQ abusing me for their business thinking that it's okay to bully an asian babe, trying to wear me out with *we are the big BULLY with broadcasting power* mentality.

Subject: It may be a FUBAR situation

I saw a new position opened 2-days ago, under the GIG OPs that looked like your masterpiece. Are you still trying to bring me in to DSIA? That won't work, with married women (CVQ) going against . . .

Some guys say that I am a God-sent babe (just like you had mentioned once upon a time), but people are trying too hard to control the situation, making the situation so ridiculously unnatural; *'we can't stand someone winning, so nobody wins (and the winner, ME, loses).'*

It's gone totally crazy, with television people dramatizing (twisting) the situation. And between recruiters trying to take my hat off at the door, LTG Rey <-> Jack Manning,, HQ <-> Engineering Group,, White <-> Black,, 26 <-> 36,, and like that wasn't enough, *CVQ (and Emeril)* has blown up the situation, *with CVQ keeps blowing & twisting the situation for their sales, and now it sounds like LTG Rey has dumped me to CVQ- (he asked CVQ to bring me in, that is)?*

LTG Rey needs your support, obviously, and if you want to help him (and want to bring me in), you would have to convince him to bring me in with DEU/MP position (instead of gambling with your contribution/ego for the GIG OPs). Being reliable is one of your merits, I know of???

Subject: Polished and Perfect

It's hard to find a good-looking, solid (modest) woman who can handle the power with generosity and good heart, especially among single women. Married women seem to be more mature, in general, but most of them seem to be either overbearing or abusive (and mean & cheap towards good-looking single females; lucky if they are not NASTY).

Funny how single women are not mean towards married women, but married women are so mean towards single women. Moms are tougher and more mature, but they are bitches, I gotta say.

I was stupid-arrogant showing off how good I was when I was with Lockheed Martin, and I learned not to be overbearing from the Lockheed

HR Director, who was very modest; he is one of the best (most mature) guys I've met in America. There was another one like him, one of the old DSIA Directors, who retired some time ago, tough and modest with good heart. Kind outside (tough inside with strong moral discipline) vs. tough outside (kind inside with big heart) was the difference, maybe.

Jerry is another good guy, with good heart and good attitude, who always provides a solution (instead of passing stupid judgment that doesn't do any good, which most people do). He is the most advanced guy I've met, but he is still always willing to listen to others and learn from it. Very clean (I look dirty next to him).

Some people say that Jerry & I are perfect together. We do have many same traits, and some women are very jealous of me having Jerry around (referring him as JACKPOT),for good reasons; He is as good as having 1000 guys around, really.

People refer me as the **GREAT ONE** *(possibly as the GREAT ONE- by some people), and one way to bring me down is money,* as they can't shake me down mentally. I know exactly where I stand and feel comfortable with my stance, NOT comfortable (unjustifiable) with where I am though financially.

I seem to be caught in the *"STU-CULOUS" POWER FIGHT* between DSIA (Military) and CVQ; STU-CULOUS (Stupid and Ridiculous) is the word used by some CVQ customer to punch what CVQ is doing . . . I hit both of them hard, I guess, and CVQ seems so wrapped around me (as another TV star said, "GET YOUR OWN SHOW!"). It's interesting to see how people talk about me, good or bad, but *CVQ is pretty DIRTY-. Play*

CHEAP can be their motto,,, and for my case, CHEATING---. Their boss calls it, ripping me off, as "smart eating."

America may be the land of opportunity, but it's not all that generous, fair, or open towards the advanced-minority -- Too many people are against the minority to excel, that is. Thought I would make a SES one day. There is no reason why I can't (except the color of my skin). Instead, I've become a **beggar**, HA HA (soooooooooo ridiculous, it makes me *laugh*)!

I kept thinking and hoping that GOOD (clean, smart, nice, fun-loving, etc.) will win, one way or another, and at the same time, can't help wondering that's me and how come I am in the losing position here???

Some CVQ show mom-hosts were even talking about removing Jerry . . . Then one night, one of the fashion jewelry designer (a former talkshow host) said, "**Look out!**" to camera (me). I often watch her show as she has very interesting & exciting personality, and also she makes me laugh with her wise and bold comments. She often talks to the camera, making specific comments about me, to me . . . It sounded like she was trying to warn me that Jerry was in trouble.

I checked with Jerry (he is referred as "eye" for his business development work), and he said that he was out of Northrop Grumman due to out of funding for his work, and he joined a British company. He assured me that it had nothing to do with me, and he was getting paid well by the new company.

I am just dumb-found, don't know what to think any more . . . . .

YOU BET! It amazes me how quick you are, grasping the **point**, without really understanding the situation, not even fully understanding my e-mails.

CVQ dramatized me, blowing me up on the air, and that generated their customers' interest,,, When I stopped testing with CVQ, they didn't just let me go away . . . . They started to hijack my e-mails, against my will. Now my e-mails not only get distributed to CVQ customers but also to other television stations (and maybe to some others). It seems like the whole America is reading my e-mails . . . .

I knew that CVQ was listening to my phone calls, both home phone and cell phone, and watching me watch their shows as well. I also learned that they could see my remote control movement. Apparently, a "light" gets turned on when I am watching their shows. One of their vendors read my remote control movement to me as I played with it :).

Now the News channels watch me, displaying different attitudes, some try to say that they are watching me as a potential danger (like watching a Hurricane blow or **911**:emgergency), some are just out of curiosity (to adapt my idea on television), and some other Live TV Shows may just watch me to stay competitive, more or less, I assume.

Anyway, it's not me trying to organize a BIG GANG. The CVQ was interested in doing that for the potential male customers--- that doesn't work, a CVQ's stupid idea. Now they are just fascinated by me, or more like moms at home demand to know what's going on with me . . .

CVQ people were babbling about the DSIA Director asking the CVQ to support me financially, with the bottom of the screen pay guaranteed. Some even told their customers that I would be joining the CVQ soon . . .

I contacted the CVQ and they just tried to threaten me to keep my mouth shut (thinking that they are the big bully and it's fine to abuse a helpless asian girl), then some proudly said on air, "We muted her." As a matter of fact, CVQ is trying to prove that they are the BIG BULLY of ALL (we can beat Military, stupid/crazy ego trip!).

I am getting totally cornered here, and my life is totally out of order now (delinquent bills, credits all screwed/no credit card, , etc. etc.). Your help (even if you can afford) wouldn't do me much good. That's like pouring a little bit of water in a JAR with a big hole.

I need a BIG HAND to survive (or die . . .). Many American women (married and single) are interested in becoming the **DEVIL**, but their attitude is like *'give me your FIVE and die.'* (huh?????)

I am open to sell my FIVE to American woman (1st choice), but I am not sure if anyone is interested in paying for! One GOOD candidate in America is Dr. Denese, but because she is from Hungary, people are making an issue, *"Made-in-America" (not made-in-america)!* Now, some anchor women seem to be interested, but I don't know their intention?

There may be others who are much better than me, but I am the one selected based on the natural result ("touchdown") due to the DoD work and being in the male-dominated environment, I guess.

$1 Million is the price some people mentioned at a Talk Show (it's fair considering the House DIVA, Martha Stewart, is a billionaire). I am open to sell it at less price (auction).

Otherwise, FIVE will just die with me. No free-giving away of what I have earned and paid for, getting harassed and beat for being selected,, not to mention being deprived of other job options, getting totally poor.

For what??? For being well-educated and preferred by men???? I would bet if I don't make it, those who want to steal my FIVE off will not make it, either;;; It will be just a bad cult of victimizing the one selected, no matter what color of skin one may have . . .

Subject: HUUUU~~~ (Dragon Breath)

Why me??? I am the most advanced single female professional in the DoD IT field, that's how people considered me as, anyway. And I seem to excite people, whether I am at work place or just hanging around not doing much. People notice me, for some reason.

It's not so much a case of the Asian elite female, it's more of the case of a single female in the advanced field. It's just that I happen to be an Asian, and people who haven't passed my skin color seem to make a MAJOR issue out of it (the easiest way to mobilize others against me).

Tonight Show is one of my favorite shows, and Jay Leno's guests seemed to be very interested in the Back Hat (or the idea of being the "FACE"). Some of his guests, female Hollywood stars, seem to wish to decorate themselves as the Face of the Earth. Some talked about what race should be the back (yellow back, etc.), some joked about the military back (Air force bathroom, etc.), and some seemed to think that I am too tall and clean for that (selected to be the Generals' back, etc.).

People on this show talk do all kinds of things about my case; Some guy guest walking around like a German general (with his hand on his rib, hand positioning down-way),,, and there was an Indian guy performing a stand-up comedy about Mercedez Benz, how it was so safe that even an Asian could drive,,, etc. etc.

Everybody recognizes my quality and seems to think that I am a good person. Nevertheless, it's annoying (a very sore spot) for many women that I (Asian) am the FIVE, and those wannabe's (females who wish to be in my shoes, IMAGE) seem to want to kill me off.

Good and solid Americans embrace the other kinds with good quality. Also, there are many who *refuse* to see good quality in other races all together (even if they see, they don't admit or change it 180 degree around). Now I have more people who feel intimidated by me, and that's the tough barrier. Majority of people who don't know me just try to determine or lead the situation based on my skin color.

Many DSIA people probably feel threatened by me (most people don't welcome those who are higher than themselves). *DSIA is having tough situation, with the Blacks (and recruiters) insisting on them leading the back, playing the choker (hassle).* DSIA has many Blacks, at least 20-30%, and that's not a small portion to ignore.

Several years ago, I heard a young girl whispering to her Mom, looking at me, "She looks like dragon breath"! And that's exactly what I seem to have become, **the Dragon Breath for the BACK!**

Subject: Extraordinary Women in America

I am the poorest FAMOUS person in America. My old boss told me that the best thing you can do is to be yourself, and that's what I've been doing,,,, Worked pretty well until I got selected as the DEVIL!

It must be the toughest job in America!!!!! I am just sooooooo surrounded by people who try to get something out of me (out of my IMAGE, that is, since I don't have anything else). Lucky to find a few extraordinary people who don't try to get something out of me (or beat me down) and just be a good friend . . .

The DSIA DIRECTOR tried to reprimand those who was trying to ride on me (to steal the back without bringing me in) to correct the situation, but apparently, those who are playing with cheap tactics have no intention of following the rule -- That's why they are playing with cheap tactics to begin with . . .

Anyway, I seem to be the only one who survives, "Made-in-DoD with Top Secret Clearance" and besides, I am natural. Nothing beats that! What I need is financial support (gotta eat), but because of those narrow-minded and/or jealous, not to mention control freaks, it goes nowhere! *(I can't have it, you can't have it---,,, I am miserable, you can't be happy---,,,).*

Many American women, especially Whites, seem to feel **sore** about me, for being more advanced than themselves, being minority, foreign-borns/raised. Singles are more dedicated to their work in many cases (ex: Dr./Secretary Rice), but too many people are trying to beat me playing with #s. WAY too much number games here,,,,

There are many extraordinary women in America, from those in politics and in media to CEO's and Directors in the industries . . . . .

Hillary Clinton, Secretary Rice, Martha Stewart . . . .
Oprah Winfrey (Talkshow Queen)
Katie Couric (1st TOP Evening News Anchor Woman)
Dr. Denese (GOOD, *married and not made-in-america*) . . . .
CHAN (GOOD, *minority* and *not made-in-america*) . . . . .

*Apples are apples, and potatoes are potatoes; *FUJI apple* ---> *potatoes soup? Does that work?*
*'*My benefit at someone else's expense'* attitude; that's not being smart, that's being *cheap*.
Negative traders trying to beat someone better than themselves in wrong ways, *making noises/troubles* (for those who offer a solution-).

Varieties and winners are what make the World interesting, providing options and the reason to choose the option . . . . ? 'Responsibility is what makes one great' and hope (or something to look forward, progress or fun) is what gets one going . . . The energy sources . . . . .

The woman who is the energy source for women, Oprah Winfrey, is the biggest media/TV star, making $260 million a year. The woman who is the energy source for men, ME, have to worry about what to eat (some even want to kill me), between jealousy and ego-fight. People will jump up and down if I make $100,000 a year.

Some people seem to think that Oprah Winfrey and I are alike. I see the similarity in the eyes, maybe, the strong sparkle, besides being single minority women. People seem to see my eyes being deep (not someone to be taken lightly).

People say I look legal, sexy, mesmerizing, and have p~erfect lips (communication skill), **Awesome**, in a word. The big issue they make is the fact that I am an Asian who grew up in another country, "not made in America."

Oprah has LOTS OF ENERGY to generate energy for women, and I have no energy to generate energy for men, for obvious reason; Star vs. Ssandbag (not a very good motivation-).

What's wrong with this picture!? People say that both Oprah and I are perfect at what each one is doing, bright and advanced, making the WAVES . . . . However, the reward is the just the opposite.

WHO wants to be in the position of being the energy source for men?

My voice is so loud (like I am SCREAMING with a HUGE SPEAKER) that I have to restrict myself from sending e-mails (and saying personal things). There are people who criticize me based on what I said in my personal e-mails, *What a PAIN!!!!!!!,,,,,*

Somehow, I seemed to have become a "Special One," and being special is not exactly easy or desirable. People get jealous or annoyed, making *negative noises* for whatever I do,,,,, and besides, new kind just upsets the old generation, not to mention that I am a stinking foreigner. Those who try to support me get cornered by those dowdy patriots abusing the race factor. People refer me as a Mercedes-Benz (because of Jerry), but I am more like a Jaguar, I think. My old friend told me years ago that I was a Jaguar, anyway.

There are shrewd people like you,,, and there are just clean people like me who go by the book (often become the victim of the dirty/abusive people, as you said). People here think I am TALL, and if I am, that's because I have strong belief that I am doing the right thing. I need to learn to make a good compromise between what's RIGHT and what's SMART though.

Good intention is the KEY. Having some fun at work place is good, even productive, I've learned, but because of those who try to abuse it (or making a victim out of a good-looking females\), even try to prevent a good-looking females from advancing to the next level;;;

Besides, the Whites and Blacks are fighting over WHO is going to head the BACK, *ganging-out- each-other*! It's not only the Whites<->Blacks, it's torn between the Military<->HR, married<->single, men<->married women, which building (HQ1)/group-,,, all kinds of *ego-fight* between different groups///

Moms can advance (to the SES level, in Government, and they have) if she is competent,,, but somehow everyone seems to have difficulty with the idea of good-looking single females advancing to a higher level\.

I've been married before, as you know, to one of the nicest guy who carried me around on his shoulder, literally,,, but it didn't seem enough (a lot of room for something else, especially when you have no kid or kids are all grown-up).

So, I tried to find some other path, more interesting path (I was hoping for . .), and it's not going anywhere because of married women insisting on everyone getting married/their kind only (one reason). I wish they allow room for others (alternative) . . . Some of them almost look like that they try to make everyone miserable just as they are. More open-minded ones think about their daughters future/option, but majority of them seem to just limit the situation to themselves; "me, now."

Too hard dealing with 10-different groups/10-different preferences, with my kind only (no others-) attitudes. Everyone is different. Some are more talented for specific things (a few are born to be the leaders or initiators, my old Lockheed Martin Boss told me), and some are more fit for specific purposes.

I just work on what suits me best, minding my own business/preference. I don't try to cut off the others who have different preference (more like try to support that, if I can).

You are much wiser than me, and I listen to what you tell me; "Soo-daa" is good for releasing the stress,,, but I don't even have that privilege these days (a prisoner of words, fart!). You can still tell me whatever you want to say, good or bad ("jaan-so-ri" is okay, sometimes GOOD) . . . . . .

There are people here who seem curious about you, my BIG SISTER (^*^). Mike DiAndrea said that you looked just like me, years ago,,, but you are actually prettier than me (I am sexier than you though :P); Ruby vs. Tanzania, maybe??? Ladyish vs. Tomboyish,,, Elegant vs. Cool,,, Shrewd (just smart) vs. Clean (too smart/"heot-ddok-ddok"),,, Snake vs. Dog (kil kil). Your people skill is remarkable, much better than me, for sure (amazes me, as a matter of fact..).

I heard a married TV weather-woman trying to twist you as someone who may have troublesome home-life. That's people. What's interesting is that people reflect themselves through others. There are all kinds of people in this world (good, bad & ugly), and those who are below your level are going to be ridiculous no matter what you do, trying to bring you down below their own level.

It is pretty amazing how you were able to jump into the working world, even in other country, at your age, after having been just a housewife for so long, not working. And now, you are running around the Asian world in your business trips, in your old age,,, after having raised two sons beautifully (even a PhD+++), experienced the European lifestyle in

France, and now the General Manager for a Chinese export firm. That's really WOW! We (our brothers and me) know what you were able to accomplish with your people skills, raising two sons and supporting your husband. We used to joke how you are a Typhoon ("TAE-POONG" as in "Chi-Maa-Baa-Raam).

I don't know why you think that I was/am closer to our brothers (vs. you). It's you who I talk more than anyone, ask for help, and depend on. I am just not pouring my guts out on you these days because everyone reads my e-mails. It's not helping me screaming my guts out with HUGE SPEAKER and not pretty when it gets reflected.

I feel like SCREAMING, ARRRRRRRRRRRRRRRRRRRRRRRRRRRRRR!

Subject: WAVE~~~~~

It's one thing to watch TV (mindlessly),,, it's a whole new experience to be watched by TV and listening to them talking to/about you (pretty interesting). Most people have very little ground on my case, and they are just playing around with my case to make the show a little more interesting, show business.

I am trying to sell my FIVE to TV people (IMAGE is their game),, but nobody seems to be interested in buying it, just a bunch of hitch-hikers, who try to ride on the **CHAN WAVE** . . . . . There are bunch of Chan Traders-, too, of course.

Only those who have their feet firmly on the ground (like Jerry & me) make wave, and those who try to ride on the wave are shaky; they change their attitudes 180-degree (or 89.4835-degree), depending on the others who are as ungrounded as they are (and whether it COSTS them something or not) . . .

My wave has moved the center stage from Washington DC -> Philadelphia -> New York -> California . . . And as it moves, it becomes bigger (image-wise) and the ground gets weaker, I see . . . New Yorkers seem better, in general; at least they don't try to hitch-hike (that's for the low-life cheapies).

I am not getting anything out of all this noises and shows . . . Watching TV (Live shows) is a lot more interesting these days, but it is also tiresome and even gives me stress (vs. relaxing,,, when you watch TV mindlessly). I have to be careful choosing the shows, too, as people try to make something out of me watching their shows,,, displaying special gestures or comments (because of my presence) . . . . .

It's always interesting to hear individuals' genuine opinions, but many seem to say what they think their viewers or customers want to hear. I need some highly-advanced filtering skills to see what's genuine. Maybe it will be easier just hearing what I want to hear; bias -> bias -> . . .

Economics 101: Demand <=> Supply; big-for-big, small-for-small, high-for-high, 2-for-2, 3-for-3. *No sense insisting on selling something that nobody is interested in buying.. Or try to prevent someone from buying what he/she wants, if they can afford..*

WHO is interested in buying **WHAT** is what matters and works!

Also, Benefits> Costs, you do,,, otherwise, no. No 3/No 2, for sure. No High/No Low (vice versa).

Someone told me years ago that I was too smart for my own good. What's wrong with being smart!? Being smart is fine, but being too smart is bad? What is being too smart, smarter than you? I'm having trouble figuring out what's being "just smart" for my own good . . . ?

A laughing baby gets kicked around for annoying and a crying baby only gets spanked!!

Subject: Portuguese Engineering

These days, people here kept leaving me bad taste in my mouth. I am so darn disgusted by people being so ridiculous and unreasonable that my spirit is WAY DOWN, right now . . . . .

American moms are interested in being the back, watching my moves & listening to me these days. The bad part is that CVQ host-moms are trying to kill off singles to win the back. Another possible road for their daughters. More options, better chance of happiness or success or whatever your heart desires.

I am very tired of everyone playing DIRTY, being so darn cheap. I've been fired up to air (television) because I was going nowhere with DSIA (for over 2-years),,, and what I see is that the air people try to steal the BACK from me, then try to use DSIA (Military) as an excuse why they can't support me-----. Who is dirtier is the question . . . . ?

It's crazy how people have fun with my stealed e-mails and learn things from my e-mails, then try to pick on me, even for being clean, referring me as penguin, getting annoyed by me being clean, too (those with bad intention). I did not ask anyone to hi-jack or read my e-mails. As a matter of fact, it's just hassle and **cost** *to me, like giving free lessons, at the expense of my* privacy- and getting punched . . . .

I've gone through soooooooo much trouble, heading the BACK, which I didn't volunteer, getting beat all the time. That's how I've become so TOUGH!!!!!! I get to see so much ugly sides of people that it's changing me from being an easy-going and fun-loving person into a stiff and cynical person.

One interesting thing about living in America is that you get to meet all different races and nationalities. I have met a number of Indian ("In-Do") engineers, some holding high positions in the engineering field. There are some Japanese Engineers holding the top positions at the top research organization, as well.

People refer me as egg (egghead => brain-oriented people, like engineers). In the world, based on my personal experience, Germans seem to be the most egg-like people. It's really a matter of each individual, but Germans are known for engineering and the best-engineered cars in the world (best-engine) are German cars; Mercedes-Benz, BMW, Audi, etc., known for superior performance and being sturdy. They are sharp, almost too sharp (kinda scary).

Emeril of Emeril Live (a famous cooking show on TV) always says "Portuguese Engineering" whenever something doesn't work well. Italians tend to be hot-headed, friendly, "gee-boon-paa" like Koreans. I was somewhat hot-headed (showing stupidish outbursts here & there, thinking I was HOT) years ago, but I may have become more like a German over the years (maybe from hanging around Jerry?).

How do you know that you may be too much? That's when you "know for sure" that others (your friends or allies) are trying to mislead you intentionally (kidding). It's hard to like people who try to abuse you (and I feel like everyone is trying to abuse me, feeling my heart getting emptied).

Subject: In Trouble

My television is not working all of a sudden. It's not broken or anything since I can see the program menu's, but no screen (it's all black). I am guessing that they have reprogrammed my receiver not to receive any signals from TV stations, like they had programmed my receiver to send signals when I am on => the air people have kicked me out, for opening my mouth about what they were trying to do, maybe . . . . .

Or it may be because of the time I sent the last e-mail to you (one minute determines the life and death); that's how crazy it is, around me,,, TOTALLY RIDICULOUS!

Too much is worse than not enough. Does that mean *the hypo's (=hypocrites) are worse than the idiots?*

The world is made of all kinds of people, and that's what makes the world interesting. Even within the same race or same field, there are all kinds of people, and I always appreciate the diversity.

Show business people and engineers are almost the opposite kind of people (drama vs. logic basis). I haven't paid close attention to show business people before, and now I kinda watched them more closely,,, and I see how they seem to think differently, to begin with. I guess I am a little more dramatic than the average engineers, and that's why I have gotten this close to them. Pretty amazing . . . Me & show business people?? Who would have even imagined that?

Even engineers and sales/marketing people in the same IT field have difficulty with each other; some engineers just can't stand the sales people. I get along well with Jerry well because he is more engineer-oriented marketing guy (business development, to be exact), and I am more customer-oriented engineer (vs. engineer-engineer who likes to dig the nitty-gritty details).

I am afraid of sending e-mails to anyone here, whose e-mails may get hijacked against their will and get exposed to everyone (and get kicked around). Who needs their private life being watched with a magnifying glass? Nobody I know, not ME, either. Dirty people are much more eager to abuse it than to praise it, for sure. The Dirties make the cleans "dirty" or "squeaky-clean."

I am actually amazed at myself,,, for being able to chit-chat like this,,,,,, despite all the money troubles that I have and a possible danger. In this material world, no money, no life (life gets screwed), everything is a drag.

Like that wasn't enough, I get jerked by air, turning my television service off??? It's not because my payment is delinquent. What's next? Starved to death? Good thing that I am a born coolie (which may be annoying to some, probably).

Subject: Human GPS

I've been trying to restrict myself from sending e-mails to you as my e-mails get hi-jacked *by CVQ* . . . . The absurd thing is that people seem to get annoyed by me chatting with my sister in China. *I did NOT ask anyone to hi-jack my e-mails to my sister (or vice versa)* . . . My sister is a BIG talker, almost unbelievably talkative. She can yak at least 10 times more than the average woman, even have a nickname "Wang-Soo-Da" (=King Yakker), very pretty, very cute, and very wise.

As you know, I have Top Secret Clearance issued by the OPM, in Sep 05, valid for 5-years at least, if not for 10-years (can be extended for 10-years, downgrading it to Secret Clearance; lockheed security people had done that, instead of re-investigating my background, as I didn't need TS clearance for my work there). An OPM investigator interviewed a DSIA employee, DSI investigator interviewed you, I believe, and another OPM investigator (a very experienced "Special Agent") interviewed ACIS

DATMS Manager and a few others,,, prior to interviewing me; He interviewed me, twice, actually. He knew my sister and her husband were in China (had lived in France before that), and my other family members were in Korea. He asked me about them, as a matter of fact, their jobs, how often I get to see them and things like that.

Why am I saying this to you? Someone hinted me that *someone is trying to use the fact that I talk to my sister in China frequently against me, making some kind of security issue*, possibly trying to use that as an excuse why I can't join Tony Montemarano's group? It's getting pretty ridiculous, to say the least.

I've just applied for another position with DSIA today, under GES group, but this group may be reluctant to bring me in because of my GCCS work (GES group considers me as 15- for my GCCS work). For other groups, such as the new Spectrum group, I don't even meet the qualification requirements. The Spectrum group has a women Director, who came from CISCO recently.

I do not wish to be the human GPS system, which I seem to be used as,,,,, it's not helping me, just costing me inconvenience and privacy, not to mention people getting annoyed that an Asian is the human GPS system.

YOU SHOULD BE THE HUMAN GPS SYSTEM (Or find someone else who may be a better GPS System) FOR AMERICA! *i don't need people getting upset at me, causing me trouble, at my inconvenience and privacy expense!* **always-always**

Sorry, again, I know how frustrated you must be with my situation here. I don't know why I have to be in the position of having to say sorry to you, over and over,,,,,

Everyone knows my quality, and that's the *problem* to many. My quality is too high, higher than 90% of people,,, and those who are below my quality are trying to bring me down,,,, playing the bullshit games; excelling quality, education- *(money-----).*

My television service is back (after three days of darkness, playing my new MahJongg game on my laptop). When I moved back to Pennsylvania from Washington DC, I didn't have the television connection for several months. I didn't watch much TV in Washington DC and didn't see the need, until I got really bored,, in the long process of joining DSIA (moving back to Washington DC). Thought that was given, and it was just a matter of getting a right (approved) position! The book-smart naive-idiot me thought that everyone would follow the rule. HA!

Now I know better, it's still the boot practice to follow the rule. Dirty (or sticky) people try to force you to break the rule, and then they get you for breaking the rule. And for me, 90% of people will be out to get me, for breaking the rule!

One's quality, once developed, is always there. The quality of life can be brought down with money. And for that, I don't have much motivation, as I have been disappointed too much;;; One gets motivated when one gets rewarded for good quality (not punished for good quality).

And that's probably the big difference between moms and singles. Having someone to protect makes moms tougher. Moms live for their children, no matter what the situation is, but singles question, "for what?" That's how I feel, anyway.

I am just feeling bad for Mom, you, our brothers (and kids), for having a daughter/sister who is too much for her own good. I want to make sure that Mom feels comfortable with me (my future), but I don't know how?

Mom told me how she trusts me doing what's best for myself,,, and sometimes I think that Mom is hanging in there, to make sure/waiting to see that I am OK? Am I a bad daughter or a good daughter, I wonder????? Probably too complicated for her to understand? Not a very helpful daughter, for sure.

Sorry, I keep dragging you down with my stinky situation,,,,,

Subject: Eyes Wide-open

Woke up early this morning, wondering, 'should I' (why I need to get up)? Who (or what) needs me or appreciates me? A hope/goal is the reason for getting up in the morning, I guess.

I want to drop everything here and go to new place (seen too much-----). I have feeling that these TV people are going to keep watching me, not with the good intention of helping me,,, but more with the negative intention, to wear me out.

What makes me really SAD is Jerry. He is the most energetic, friendly, clean GUY, who I have met, and he seemed to be WAY DOWN (so unlike him), with what he had to deal with (around me/moms-HIM--- for him being single preferring single females). *HOW RIDICULOUS!*

As you've been saying, in this material world, money is the security, and that's what many are trying to make sure that I don't have (just purely out of "sim-tong" for some, and for some others, it's a way to kill me, I suppose). I am going to die from hunger here; I know that for sure now.

I should have left here years ago, but I kept hoping that something would work out, being the most beloved/popular female here; *Didn't know that the ONE who gets the most votes loses in this case . . . One who gets too many votes even dies . . .*

I almost felt like I was dead today, absolutely no energy for a while,,,,, but I am trying hard to give myself strength to start over . . . . If DSIA was like New Orleans hit by the Hurricane Katrina (me), as someone said,,, I, too, was like the New Orleans hit by the Hurricane Katrina myself!

What I am going to do is to sell my furniture and move back to Korea. I can be a good English Teacher for professionals (adults), I guess, and I may do very fine. I am the teacher's proud and beloved daughter, after all (excelling in school, being the top of my class, "mo-beom-sang" me).

There is no money in this old town house. I had refinanced it to eat, and now I am behind the mortgage payments (=>the mortgage company can take over the house). I gotta sell my furniture anyway, to eat (SIGH-). I haven't been hungry yet, but I am almost there. I am just eating what's been bought (and saved), no new food-shopping. No energy----.

I was planning to deal with it by myself, but it's too much for me to handle alone. You are tougher than me, for dealing with things like this,,,,, I hope? Very SORRY for putting you through my CRAPPY SITUATION! I don't know what I am supposed to do???

My e-mails probably frustrate the hell out of YOU, even make your heart *JUMP* these days, and that's NO FUN-, no help--, no doubt. You put up with it, I know,,, trying hard to encourage me, as my BIG SISTER, no need to say . . . . .

Some people connect me with Germans (referring me as Mercedes-Benz, I guess), and I had a Jewish guy BITCHING about me-, last night, on a TV talk show. This talk show comes right after the Jay Leno's Tonight Show on the same channel, and is hosted by an Irish guy; I watched it a few times, and you wouldn't believe how his guests would attack him or make fun of him for his last name (in conjunction with me).

It's really tiresome when so many people are out to get YOU--- (you as in someone in general, ME, that is). I try hard to ignore that, but that itself is a big effort on my part.

People who don't know me just determine their attitude based on their own prejudice (or benefit/interest), and that's it! What I do makes no difference. High-brow females are not very popular (annoying to many), and in my case (being an asian) makes it much worse.

Many women get annoyed by **ME or** ME (naturally),,,, men could use several ME,,, but since there is only one ME, making one or two guys happy, those who don't have something better (jealous/annoyed) play the traders-(959-).

Men kick out 19-, just like women kick out 16- (EGO), even between the same race-. Don't get noticed is what's going on here (except maybe some stupid ones) - - - -

Subject: 4 Symbol, blessing+ or curse-?

I have several items listed on eBay to sell. It's soooo RIDICULOUS to have to sell everything I bought over the years, furniture and all, to EAT,,, but that's the way it is with ME right now. "Some serious Stellar CUT—" as someone said . . . .

Others who have similar education/experience own a few houses and stocks, have retirement savings, and keep moving forward (getting richer/more established, one way or another). How unfair??? It's soooooo UNEVEN for my case, men love the idea of me and women hate me!!!!!

Cheers from guys, and hatred from many women . . . More reasonable women support the "natural" click,, but there are so many who are just negative, *one way* or *another*. It makes me think that there are many who are dissatisfied with their lives here. If you are content with your life, what others do wouldn't matter. It's none of your business, unless they are out to get you,,, but so many seem to operate just based on their "tummy hurts-" (=sim-tong).

*Overall, too many people are playing the rock (vs. water); my way (group) only, at someone else's expense-. It must be the hardest job on Earth, as someone said . . . . There are sooooooooooooooo much **mumbo-jumbo's** going on here, I don't know what to think (and don't even want to know) any more. Nothing natural or genuine, just full of bullshits and bad tactics; I am not sure which one is worse?*

*Some are even trying to pick something out of us talking,,, like you & I are discussing the world politics or something. **We need to synchronize our clocks to discuss the world politics**, I think, that's the most important factor . . . .*

Some people refer Jerry and me as the Zebra couple . . It's a nice idea that seems to appeal to many women, but men have very different view. I have not talked to Jerry for a while as moms here seem to jump up and down when I contact him. In fact, they try to break us apart because their tummy hurts. *I am just totally dumb-found by the level of their ganging-up bullshit!*

I am learning to play wise now, how to balance between 'knowledge is power' and 'not knowing is the medicine.'

It looks like the whole world is watching **YOU & ME**, and it will have to
be YOU covering ME . . . .

What I would like to suggest is that YOU consider using PTI to use me;
PTI is an 8(a) company, and Chi Lee is the president there; Chi is a
former SAIC employee, and one of the two VP's is also a former
SAIC employee (Bill Goodridge). The other VP is a former Lockheed
Martin, I believe.

Chi is a nice, easy-going guy, about my age, but you can choose to work
with a VP, if you feel more comfortable with you kind (?). For me, makes
no difference; I am comfortable with all the nice, reasonable guys (or gals),
as you know . . .

As for DSIA, there is little (or no) chance for me to join; as far as I know,
Black females and /or recruiters may be interested in leading the back
there. Looks like the HR is not supporting me joining DSIA for DEU-
positions (head in),,,,, and non-DEU positions, (Black-) females cut me off
(not sure if my RED status with DSIA has been cleared?). No White
females are interested in the back position there (w/ GS-13 being the
highest);;; one got promoted to GS-14, two years ago, and she was OUT
soon after (fat attitude, possibly, annoying others incl. her co-workers,
trying to boss them around, etc.; that's what I saw, anyway).

So, it's up to YOU to get the back going outside (up to DSIA for the
Military, I suppose). I am spelling this out because some people seem to

try to make an ISSUE out of me not joining DSIA, like it's up to me, or like they are concerned with the Military well-beings.

As for the air, my impression is that they may be interested in "adapting" what's going on with the IT world, looking for good change (new movement+) . . . .? A *wrong start by CVQ (different motivation), but there is nothing you (or I or anyone) can do to change that. They are not only hijacking my e-mails, but they are also tapping my phone, I believe.*

Subject: 5 Statue

I put my portrait on eBay to get the back going, just asking for my two-year salary (bare minimum) that I was entitled to but deprived of because of the ganging-up's (injustice), but it went nowhere. In fact, the eBay kicked me out-! That's exactly the kind of *crazy* situation that I have to deal with here . . . .

Anyway, Moms are out to get ME---- (and other new Babes-), so they can play the back at work (WHO wants that-!!!!!!!!!!!! SIGH-) . . *Some guy was joking about having the Martha Stewart tattoo on his ass.* Single females are not interested in being the back any more;;; you get noticed, you get killed (WIN -> LOSE/). Even if you win the guys, the best is to get used to kick off some other younger babes . . . *Okiedokie, that's grrreat-!) . . .*

Even between men, 3-guys insist on 36 only, and the most managers think that they are pain for managing,,, unless he is 19 . . . And 3-guys don't like the idea of a manager being 19 (the boss' babe, oops, gotta be careful/).

DSIA couldn't bring me in for almost 3-years, but they keep claiming me as their PROPERTY,,,, so now I am just 'standing at the DSIA DIREC-TOR's Office' (symbolically). **CHAN=GCCS** (Global Command and Communications System) -> GIG (Global Information Grid).

I do feel specially about DSIA, as I had great experience working there before (the best experience of all, flying around the world, "being at the right place, at the right time"),,, but that's the very reason make others RESIST ME (+++++++ and -------- at the same time) now.

You may be laughing at this (or think it's a ridiculous comparison), but some people compare me with Marilyn Monroe: Hollywood star vs. IT Industry engineer? Some people even see me as an Asian Jackie K-(O)-, and they DO NOT like the idea (Asian Jackie K-O is "SUPER-BAD")! A very advanced fashion jewelry designer mentioned that even Jackie K-O would be jealous of me!

It must be pretty annoying to those in show business when an egghead becomes known as 4-SYMBOL, even a stinking-minority Asian! But, hey, I didn't ask for, I just got selected, so what am I supposed to do?

PART 7
GOING GLOBAL

MOM MANAGER FACED WITH MANAGEMENT CRISIS

A very polite and friendly Indian guy, representing the Global Networking, Inc. (GNI), contacted me for a position supporting the BMI for ATM
to MPLS migration task. I called in for an interview with my neighbor's
phone because my phones were being tapped, to avoid distracting noises
and keep the interview safe.

Just as the GNI recruiter assumed, I had the perfect expertise that the
hiring manager needed, and the interview went pretty smoothly. Joyce,
the BMI Hiring Manager, was impressed with my experience, listening
mostly as I described my experience supporting the DSIA ATM Services,
which was similar to the task she needed to get accomplished. I was the
best-qualified candidate for this task, she said. She asked me when I
could start working, and I answered, "Yesterday," laughing a little,
meaningfully . . . She was a high-tech manager with BMI, so she must be
pretty advanced, I figured. She laughed, too, and said, "I am hard-
pressed with four."

Joyce was in her late 40's (maybe early 50'), stubby and stubborn looking
with strong eyes. She introduced me to her right-hand guy, Gary, who
was very tall, 6'4" or so, in his late 50's (or maybe in 60's). He looked like
a nice, easy-going guy, who was leading the network transformation task
to implement the ATM backbone and standardize the CNAGI enterprise

network interface. He looked at me with somewhat belittling expression on his face but seemed pretty pleased with the way I looked, saying, "Oh, cool . . ."

There was another GNI engineer who joined the group on the same day, Mike, who was not exactly a pleasant looking guy, generating a gloomy mood. He was going to be my partner to begin with, so I made an effort to be friendly, "Hey Mike, Wanna go lunch?" He smiled, thinking 'just as I heard . . .'

Mike and I didn't have cubicles assigned to us. We were a subcontractor to an on-site contractor who was using a relatively small space of the CNAGI building, and there wasn't any kind of HR or facility management to accommodate what new people needed. We used any empty cubicles for a week or so. Then I took a cubicle surrounded by younger guys, as Mike suggested. A big mouth Fred was on my left side and his buddy, Todd, on my right side. A cute-looking young contractor guy, Shawn, wearing a baseball hat, was across the narrow hallway. Mike took a cubicle next to Shawn. As soon as I moved to cubicle #1003, these guys called their friends to tell them about me, "We have Tina Casey here" or "She is the right-O" and talked about me among themselves, all excited . . .

Everyone in the building already heard about me, although nobody made a fuss over me. They were just watching me . . . Then one day, a friendly Black cook made a comment about my situation wondering if I was aware that some Americans (or Blacks) were trying to drive me to death. I smiled, nodding at his inquiring comment.

Joyce watched how I was interacting with Mike, with curiosity and amazement, going to lunch or whispering to each other, like old buddies. Mike didn't look like an elite guy, and he dragged his feet when he was walking, making awful sounds. Joyce sighed when she saw me walking with Mike, possibly thinking that he was a wrong match for me. Not exactly the kind who should be promoted as the top engineer, judging from the look.

Gary brought a box to my cubicle, saying, "Here's a Christmas present for you," handing me a laptop. "Oh, Okay, Thank you, there was a Christmas tree over there", I said, pointing at an artificial Christmas tree that was in the cubicle #1005, that I noticed on my first day. He laughed, "Ha Ha Ha." Apparently, some people were preparing to *Christmas baby me out* before I came on board. Mike took the cubicle #1005.

Joyce came in once or twice a week, and Gary functioned as the Manager in her absence. While Gary was more interested in me, helping me get started, Mike approached Joyce, calling her when she was not in the office, and soon, Mike became her favorite. He was quick and articulate and she started calling him and inviting him to her office to help her sharpen her technical knowledge. Her engineers never seemed to visit her office or to ask her for any kind of direction or guidance, except a fat Mexican guy with a big mouth and exaggerated arrogant attitude.

I didn't feel up to being friendly, having had a few years off, seeing so much unpleasant attacks on television and dealing with all kinds of people playing their personal games against me. I was anxious to do the work, but I was beat-up, mentally and emotionally. I sat in my cube with blank mind, trying to read project documents, just barely asking less than minimum questions to Gary. Mike diligently figured out what systems needed to be setup to function in this environment, configuring my system along with his. I just let Mike do what needed to be done to get started.

One guy who I talked was the MPLS lead engineer in Raleigh, North Carolina, Jim. Jim invited me to his MPLS meeting, and I called him to introduce myself. He was excited about my call, responding to me with "Hey, Chan!" like I was one of his old buddies. After a brief conversation, he said, "We can talk on the *sametime*." (to be more private). He sounded spunky and very guy-like with a nice husky voice.

People at my office kept clearing their throats at 11:00 o'clock sharp after I talked to Jim . . . He was a well-known and popular guy, for sure. I talked to him on the *sametime* (the BMI instant message system) for a few times, but soon I learned that my *sametime* messages were getting hijacked by the CVQ (and other television people) and stopped chatting with him after his role had been defined. Gary was the shooter, and Jim was the NP (chick cop) for the BMI . . .

A month or so later, Gary said to Mike, "She is in a well. We're gonna have to dig her up." And Mike said, "I'll dig." I felt very sad listening to their conversation, and what Mike was willing to do to save me almost brought tears in my eyes.

Gary assigned a dumb task for me and Mike, for determining what devices were alive on the network. There were thousands of devices on the list, and Mike and I had to ping those devices one by one to check which one responded and which one did not. Mike was already helping the network cutover work led by another senior engineer, Bernie, walking around the office and volunteering to help, and he didn't like this simple task. I was just fine doing this task, not having to think. This monotonous, absolute no-brainer work helped me to stay calm and relaxed, while bringing myself up for the real work, work that requires some thinking.

Fred kept making comments about every little thing I did (eating, playing with my pen, even when my stomach made tiny noises) . . . It was annoying, but sometimes, it cracked me up, for him being so ridiculously attentive of me . . . He kept complaining about Gary being "horrible (shooter)," too. Every once in a while, I responded to his comments, mostly with negative comments about unreasonable gang-bullshits (sacrificing a good looking females)! Gary and other older people were making comments about the interaction and arguing between me and the younger guys sitting around me, sending signals, playing music, clearing throats, and I started to laugh a lot. Sometimes, I had to run outside to laugh by myself, having to laugh too much. My sense of humor was returning back to me . . .

When I completed my first dumb task of pinging devices on the network, Gary assigned me as a Site Designer for the CNAGI network refresh. It surprised me that he assigned me, a scummy sub, as the site designer responsible for conducting survey, designing and coordinating the network design with CNAGI customers. I was thrilled to be treated fairly for my expertise, after all.

My mind was still pretty blank, and I sat around for a few weeks, not jumping into my new task. Then I noticed my first site, Richmond, was marked in red, stating that it was behind the schedule. I woke up, 'Oh, shoot! What am I doing?' I started working diligently, trying to figure out what needed to be done and how. I did read the *Site Planner's Guide* and remembered that it had the information I needed to get started at least. My head started to function, as those young guys commented, "The engine is coming . . ."

I suggested to Gary to develop a comprehensive site survey template that everyone could use. Gary was reluctant to support me developing a survey template (considering it as a lead engineer's task), but I developed the draft survey template as I needed. After seeing the draft, Gary became more willing to help me complete it. He was supposed to be the lead engineer, recognized the need, and I asked him to lead the development of this template with other team members (instead of me leading).

Ken, the Project Manager, a single guy located in Philadelphia, was very supportive of my survey template as well as to get the back going . . . . I gave him my blessing, as everyone was expecting me to whistle, and Wendy, a German-heritage single female at the Harford facility, who was on this project team, to be the next, as Gary hinted me . . . .

Majority of people at this BMI office were members of the Maintenance Group for the CNAGI network, responsible for the administration of various systems used by the CNAGI and the troubleshooters for these systems. The only BMI engineer was Kevin, a very quiet clean elite-like single guy. He and I were in the same project team, but before I had chance to get to know him, he was out of the office, taking 2-3 months off . . .

Joyce was trying to establish herself as FIVE, "You guys are going to support me wearing the brush, right? Ho ho ho." Everyone was quiet, and Gary responded with "A-rrrrrrrrrrrrrrrrr", irritated. She walked around talking to her engineers trying to win them to support her, but nobody supported her . . . Then one day, Bernie, Joyce's left-hand single guy, told her, "You got it!"

Next day, Joyce invited Gary, Bernie, Mike and me into her office for a meeting. Bernie showed up a few minutes late, and she got up from her chair and told him, "**SIT!**" He looked at her (trying not to show his thought of wanting to smack her for that) and stood at the door for the whole meeting. He kept looking at me while he was talking to Joyce, trying to warn me that her intention would be to officialize her seat and kick me out (wondering if I knew). I knew it, too, of course.

One thing that Joyce and I had in common was being hefty, as Fred commented, and Joyce looked like a hefty woman with tough expression on her face and chunky body even though she was rather short. I was more like hefty inside that some people could see through, not acting lightly.

Older guys in their 50's or 60's always made positive comments about me . . . "Hmmm~, oxygen" with exaggerated breathing when passing me in the hallway, the place needing two chimneys (for me being so hot), "She is only 60 minutes!" etc. etc. Joyce was trying to kick me out, going around and asking people's opinion, "No candy?" The old guys' response was, "Oh, I want the candy here . . . . "

It was a pretty relaxed group, and Joyce started coming in once a month (or when she felt she needed to be in the office in between), having to take care of her Mom going through the cancel treatment, having to take care of her son with doctor's appointments and for other personal matters. Sometimes she walked around passing some pretzels or cake for everyone and office supplies to those who needed as there was no office supplies provided for this group. She was the first woman manager who I had chance to work for, and what she was doing seemed like she was playing a Mom to keep her office (almost like a secretary).

Some people were trying to put Mike down, especially his peer BMI guys, as a no-brainy techie, commenting him as being hideous, being a stupid hyphen(-), and even tried to chase him away, literally, saying things like "You are done, buddy." Mike was an excellent troubleshooter, and after a few months, some people started referring him as a "machine," and some others referred him as a "call center" for having constant conference calls for his network cutover tasks.

Mike and I had some discussion about new MPLS techniques, and as soon as this discussion was over, Bernie, who had helped Mike get started as his assistant, came over to Mike's cubicle and warned him of 15-. Mike looked at me with a victorious and contemptuous smile combined.

Gary reminded me of one of my old DSIA friends. They generated similar mood, both with soft hearts and full of something, super friendly but trying to be arrogant with racial attitude towards me (insecure and shaken), thrilled to play the power-ball, and the exact same voice that even confused me sometimes. Fred kept saying, "This is horrible!" Fred wanted to play the power-couple with me, kept bugging me to be their "kid-O!" I responded, "kid-o-o? I am not a kid-o, go find someone else!" He whined, "You gotta help me find someone!"

For one of the sites, I was assigned as an engineer supporting Connie, a site designer. Connie was very excited about me being her engineer and invited me to her design meeting. She was new at this work and was lacking technical background to do the design work. She was no engineer, for sure.

A site survey should have been the first step, but apparently, she didn't know what information she needed to collect. She had visited site and looked around, taking some picture of the equipment room. That made me to wonder how the heck she had become a site designer to begin with? I volunteered to survey the site to collect the missing information to help her, but she didn't support me to conduct the survey for her, just dragging me along with her sloppy design process.

Connie was the big mouth of this design team, and she was brave telling the team at a team meeting about the importance of the site survey, the importance of having the picture (memory) of what the place looked like, not the importance of collecting the right information. She was claiming that she was the top designer for this group. I was new to this group, as a contractor, so I just spoke the minimum required at the team meetings.

I kept correcting Connie's design errors (questioning her design), and she finally admitted that she didn't know what she was doing, she was guessing the IP addresses and was trying to copy what other designers were doing . . . It was below muddling through . . .

<Subject: Lutherville design document>

Connie,

Your diagram is vague, and your switch configuration document seems to have several faults. First of all, you would need to clarify the connectivity diagram.

The following are unclear and/or need to be corrected:

1) The connection between the Luther3750 and VMSWLA01 is not clear. You need to specify how they will be connected and on which port on which device.

2) Where on earth does this router interface IP address 172.37.49.28 come from? You do NOT guess IP address.

3) sc0 is not a physical connection, it is the logical the interface used for TCP or UDP connections for the SNMP or Telnet connection. TCP/UDP is the transport layer of the TCP/IP or the layer 4 of OSI 7 layer that require the IP connection. If you don't understand the basics of TCP/IP and the OSI 7 layer concept, it won't do any good for me to keep explaining what you are doing wrong.

4) Router should be connected to either the port 48 of the last module of the new switch or the SUP module, not both. It will cause some problem if you have the both links up.

5) The subnet mask for your printer VLAN should be 255.255.255.240 and for the trunk it should be 255.255.255.252.

6) The printers should be distributed between the modules instead of connecting all of the printers onto one module.

There was no way that her muddled-design was going to work, and the refresh for this site was going to fail, I was pretty sure. I didn't want to be blamed for her incompetency in design work. After I helped her with her design task (which wasn't even my responsibility), Connie bitched about me being a "gun hole" or being "horrible" at the team meeting instead of thanking me. So I told her to just pass me her design when she completed.

Connie turned around and complained to Joyce that I wasn't attending her design meeting. My responsibility as the engineer was to configure the network switches based on Connie's design, I told Joyce, and I didn't want to be responsible for Connie's lack of technical knowledge to be a designer. I had to spend more time correcting her design than designing my site from the scratch. The failing part was I could only correct her design based on her wrong design, without the knowledge of the site. I wanted to stay out of the design that wasn't going to work, but Connie was trying to threaten me that we design this *TOGETHER-*.

Connie was very aggressive and didn't hesitate to play the bullshit game positioning herself as the representative of married women . . . She was broadcasting her absence to everyone in the company, about going somewhere with her doctor husband, shooting 53!!!

Mark, the CNAGI site design representative, was aware of Connie having trouble with her design task, and he was about to kick her out of the design team. I backed her up helping her with the wrong design, telling him that I was with her. He was interested in being the guy leading the back with me, and he went along with me supporting Connie . . .

Joyce realized that what she was trying to do with me, stripping the back off of me, wasn't going to work and she needed me around . . . She was a smart woman, and I tried to promote her as the back for the managers as she wished . . .

I see many moms (and Blacks) on TV,,, as the anchors, sports reporters, home shopping hosts, etc., and that's how I learn about them, their ways and mentality in general (and their attitudes toward me -or- other single females). Actually, you give me pretty good idea of how other moms may be like,,, (other than you being on my side as MY SISTER).

For what I have seen, men are more willing to compromise for the harmony than women, in the work place, more reasonable and mature, as the professionals.

There are many advanced females who people don't know about. I know some, but not everyone. Even some in Korea are very advanced, possibly more advanced than me. I don't know how my old high school friend, Young-ran, is doing these days . . . ? She was good-looking and smarter (more advanced thinker) than me, in many ways. She studied the Artificial Intelligence at Boston University, worked for the KIST for a while, and became a CEO of her own research company.

I am puzzled about the mentality of those who insist on *if not me, no one else (my way only)*. How does that work when there are 1000 different kinds of people? Some just choose to be a hassle to those who are better than themselves with nothing gained by doing that.

It's those who are bigger, open to embrace/allow rooms for others, get to pay for the small-minded people's RIDICULOUSLENESS,, kinda like a good husband pays for his bitch wife or a good wife pays for her bullish husband.

I learned some Tao the other day . . . .

* Wisdom is knowing that you are nothing, and love is knowing that you are everything (humble, and giving)

* Foolish/rigid consistency is the hobble gobbling of little mind (be open and flexible)

* Trying to control leads to ruin (control freaks screw things, for sure, trying to control the let-it-be matters)

* Live by not interfering (allow others to do/figure things their own way)

For what I've learned, I will say that Tao is based on the water nature, **soft and allowing**,,, and it's how things run smoothly (resolving conflicts, like how water softens the rough edges of rocks, I imagine . . .), makes me think of your ability to soften things around you. I was known for softening the customers in my good times, making them more open,,,

Be responsive, another good advice that I always keep in mind. Also, according to Tao, you are not controlling anything, but you are being controlled by the Universe (nature?) . . . . . As I said, *control freaks screw things, trying to control too hard,,,,, and unreasonable people screw things, being ridiculous.*

People here say that I am TALL (some say maybe the tallest-). I've always been tall, standing up for what I believe is the right thing (as Mom used to say about me). Actually, people here made me super **TALL**, by keep **cornering** me;;; When one is pushed hard against the wall, one has no choice but to stand and be TALL-. 'What doesn't kill you makes you stronger.'

TEMP NETWORK DESIGNER

I needed some help with my first design task, what processes to follow through and how to use the CNAGI IP tools. Brad was the #1 engineer for this task, and I decided to get help from him. He was located in Hartford, Connecticut, and I barely knew him, other than he had made the most comments, very cautiously, when Gary and I were developing the site survey template.

Brad walked me through a CNAGI IP tool step by step, very carefully, almost breathtakingly, until I completed all of the steps required for the design. Most guys would have helped me with some basic steps and would have let me follow through the procedures requiring the similar steps, but he was different. He went through every single step, making sure that I completed each one successfully, almost like a dad teaching a new thing to his first son. I liked him for his warmth and carefulness (his hidden desire) that I could feel through the telephone line.

I thanked Brad for helping with this training, and he said, "No problem, I like new people joining the group and asking for my help." And I quickly replied, "That's what makes the work interesting " realizing that I should not sound like I knew the working world better than him or equally well (hidden desire and all). He laughed hard, and that night, I heard some people commenting on air how that was "**I am a happy man**" laugh, the very genuine laugh bursting from the chest. Words traveled fast, and the next thing I knew was that people were talking about Brad & me as a hot couple. Brad was a German-American, and when I chatted with him on the *sametime*, it became a news noise.

The CNAGI network refresh had been performed by the site designers at the Hartford facility for a number of years. Gary was the new Task Manager/Lead Engineer at the Cherryhill facility. Kevin was the only Site Designer at the Cherryhill facility, and I was the first contractor assigned as the Site Designer and assigned to be responsible for the Disaster Recovery site along with other regular sites.

Brad was the Site Designer for the CNAGI HQ facility in Philadelphia as well as the Cherryhill Data Center in New Jersey. "I can speak for engineers, and that's a H~uge responsibility putting on one engineer," I said to Gary and suggested that the HQ refresh should be worked on by a team of 3-4 engineers. "Brad is tough, he can handle," Gary responded, proudly. And I wanted to say, 'Do you have any idea what kind of pressure you are putting on him?' but I didn't argue. Gary was the Task Manager, and it was his call. He wanted to beat us (me and Mike, the subbies) and seemed proud of having the top notch BMI engineer who was better than Mike who turned out to be super technical, "Great and good," Gary compared the two knowing that Mike would hear him (or would be listening to our conversation).

After I had a few little chats with Brad on the *sametime*, everyone was going wild about us. Connie broadcasted a "ya." e-mail to everyone, and the Project Manager eliminated Brad from his project status distribution list. I had to stop talking to Brad. He waited for me to contact him, I knew, but I was no help to him (15-).

Kevin returned to work, and he was getting very interested in me, whispering, "Oh, my God," when I was passing him, or laughing hard listening to my conversation with some other older guy, which was very unlike this classy reserved quiet guy. With Kevin back to work, the Project Manager kept pressuring Kevin and Wendy to get the back going . . .

Kevin wasn't one of those guys who would get ticked off as a power-shooter or play a bullshit game . . . He indicated that he would be interested in coupling with me only, nobody else. The Project Manager was a mean guy who tried to abuse the situation to corner the engineers (and me). Mike stood by me trying hard to protect me from this Project Manager's cheap management bullshit!

I completed my first design and asked Mike to help me doing the network cutover scheduled on Saturday. Usually, different site designer and site engineer were assigned for a site refresh, however, I was assigned to work as both the site designer and the engineer. I had configured the networking switches with Mike's help but I had never done any kind of cutover work. Mike was busy with other cutover task and he linked me with another troubleshooter up in Connecticut, Joe, who said, "Why the hell not?"

Joe had an attitude about me, obviously, but he knew what he was doing, and that was all that mattered. He was carrying on the task like a pro. The cutover task was going to last for several hours, and I was getting bored sitting in front of the telephone and said, "I am going to step out for a few minutes. Joe quickly responded, "You can step out as l~ong as you want." I laughed, "Ha Ha Ha Ha Ha~" Apparently, the television people were tapping my phone at work got my laugh and my laugh became famous, with people making up laughs on television trying to laugh like me, Ha Ha Ha Ha Ha~

After my first site refresh was successfully completed, some people assumed that I was an expert or tried to corner me as "job #1." (Someone actually made this comment on some television news). I was not an expert at this particular environment, but the Project Manager was trying to corner me as the top engineer-. Ridiculous. *He was full of it! He was trying to hook-up with me, telling others that he was doing that to get rid of me (26).. What is this!?*

Gary was rather lazy, and he needed engineers who could do the design. I was actually helping him understand what it took to be a site designer for this refresh task. And his appreciation to me was expressed as, "The bottom line is . . . ," for every conversation he had with others. Maybe he was trying to cover me in his own way, but it was more annoying than helping. I volunteered him to be the bottom for the old married women there . . . He laughed hard and played along . . . That fit him well.

I became relatively friendly with a cafeteria cook, who always seemed to try to make my sandwich with extra effort. One day he said to me, looking at Gary standing in the line, "I wouldn't say he is stupid, but he is . . . . ." I nodded, 'Yep, kinda sorta like a lazy hypocritical knucklehead who tries to be super-cool but doesn't know what he is doing?'

The BMI networking group got merged into TA&T, and a new Manager for my group came on board. Joyce got promoted as a Technical Director. The new Manager, Ron Kimbell, invited everyone for his first department meeting, and he sounded good with a well-prepared introduction speech. It was a telephone conference, just like most of the meetings were conducted as telephone conferences in this environment with members of the group scattered around the country.

After the speech, Ron asked everyone to ask questions. To my surprise, the reserved Brad jumped in to ask the first question, followed by Connie with a whole bunch of questions. Connie kept addressing the new Manager as "Hey Ron . . . " I just listened like most people, and Ron said, "We can all have Chan." Mike jumped in and said, "I will be the right person to circle back."

I stayed quiet, keeping my presence unknown, smiling behind the phone. Connie commented, "This is a hole bill," and continued to address him as "Hey Ron, This is Connie . . . " I thought she was pretty darn annoying, trying too hard to get his attention, sounding like a nuts. Ron must have run out of his patience, and the very polite Ron finally punched Connie with the word "psycho." He seemed like a straightforward kind of guy, my kind of guy.

Gary had left the group and joined CNAGI (where he came from), and the new team leader for the refresh project was Scott, the guy who used to sit next to Gary's cube. Scott was the expert on the BMI configuration management system, writing the user's guide and training new engineers how to use the system.

Ron arranged a meeting with each and everyone, trying to get to know people working for him and to get the status of each one's task. I had my first meeting with him, a little nervous of my task status (and my big name), since I was out of the design task (as the Project Manager kicked me out). Ron sounded warm and kind, and I just responded to his questions. He was interested in picking me up, saying, "I hear ya (vs. you)..

It turned out that Ron was single. I learned that right after my first meeting with him, and that was even better. He could justify himself better. He intended to get rid of me (5-), but he became interested in me after the first meeting@ as he announced to people with an email, not directly but he made himself pretty clear. He changed his Engineering group leader, initially assigned to an old project manager, a guy, to a senior woman from the configuration management group.

I was on the *sametime* all the time, day and night, even on weekends. Ken, the single Project Manager, was always on, too, including weekends. Apparently, both he and I had no better life than sitting in front of the BMI laptop. Soon after, others started hanging on the *sametime* at night and on weekends. Even Joyce signed onto the *sametime* on Thursday night.

Ron was on the *sametime* all night long on Wednesday night, the day I had my first meeting with him. I was on all night long with him, too, of course. He kept hanging on the *sametime* at night, then he took a few days off to take care of some personal business (and to clear his head@). When he came back, he was on the *sametime* all night long on Saturday and Sunday, and I was looking at his name all weekend and all night long, falling for something.

On Monday, I heard a radio station on my way to work saying, "He is trying to blow up, Ha Ha Ha~" I used to wake up every morning with the radio station announcing my back status as, It's *Michaelangel*, It's *Michaelangelo, Michaelanchello,* then back to *Michaelangel, Michaelangelo, Michaelangel, Michaelangelo, Michaelanchello-, Michaelangel* . . .

A few days later, I heard a radio station announcing, "It's Gordon" on my way to work.

I am doing very well as you may hear through the grape vines . . . ? Some people may consider me as the most fabulous (and envied/hated) professional woman in America these days.

Many people refer me as a "SHARK" because of my DoD work background. The air is still after me, hi-jacking my work e-mails and tapping my work phone, and my building lights are flickering sometimes when the air is attacking . . . .

All this attention is pretty exhausting, mentally,,, after I have already been dealing with all kinds of people playing all kinds of games for so long. I can use some break,,,, but people wouldn't leave me alone, so I keep playing . . . .

Last Wednesday (12/26) morning, on my way to work, I noticed on the New Jersey highway that everyone was driving their cars with the headlights on . . . Puzzled me for a few minutes, then I was wondering whether I should turn my car headlights on or not. I didn't because one of my car headlights needs to get fixed.

Television people are joking about New Jersey now for picking me up, being too clean or being righteous, going against the Thursday Washingtonians, possibly. Who would be the Tuesday people, I wonder, New Yorkers or maybe the up-in-the-air people?

New York is definitely very exciting, and I always enjoy visiting New York. It's never like the NY tour I had with you, just short trips. New

York is referred as big apple (apple = high class). New Jersey is thought of as egg state (egg = brain), Idaho would be the potatoe state, I guess, and California may be orange state. Florida is supposed to be orange state, too (a backup orange state)?

Speaking of New York trip, let's plan a trip we (Mom, you and me) can take together, possibly in September or October? Many people say Turkey is an excellent place to visit, very different than any other places. You check and pick the tour package and let me know. Like Mom, I need something to look forward to, really, really, really. My new passport has no stamp! SUCKS! My old passport had many interesting stamps and all kinds of stickers, and I loved it! That made me feel like I was LIVING, FLYING the world,,,

Now, I am not sure if I have the energy to fly from America to Europe, then back to America, then to Korea right after,,,, I was young and restless, and pretty darn lucky, I must say. Guess those were my happy spring years. People always say that I have a lot of energy, but my mind keeps sinking these days.

I heard a TV anchorman referring me as "Dr. Madonna!" Is that 8??? These days, people often refer me as "Dr." for my professional skills (vs. "Dr. Chan" as Jerry referred for being likable). Some says I am the "Master 3 Artist"! I do have the MENSA IQ, and that's why I had chosen to become an engineer to begin with . . . And people here, men, seem to think that I am gorgeous. The BMI woman manager seem to think I am gorgeous, too! Our brothers will be laughing hard, HA HA HA~ How could my sister be gorgeous!?#%&

WORKING AT DOWNTOWN PHILADELPHIA

With the BMI Networking group merging into TA&T, the CNAGI/BMI New Jersey facility where I was working got closed down. Some of the refugees including myself had been given some work space at the CNAGI HQ building in Philadelphia. The BMI refugees had to share cubicles, one cube for three or four people, so I didn't need to (couldn't) go to office every day, just once a week. Whenever I showed up, the guards at the lobby got excited, whistling and going, "Woo~ Hoo~"

I took the train to go to work, and it was interesting to use the public transportation. People on the train made different gestures when they saw me (somehow they noticed me, or guessed it was ME who was making the 4 wave), and the conductors for the train shouted **University City** (or changing it to **University Step**) when the train neared the University of Pennsylvania station.

Being in the center of Philadelphia was pretty exciting. I felt lively with many shops and many people walking around . . . I had always worked at some quiet suburb areas, and lately I hadn't even visited any city. I walked around the downtown Philadelphia during the lunch time, like a country-girl who had been living at some remote area for all her life: getting free drinks, eating hot sausage, and checking things around . . . .

I was given a new task working as a Technical Administrator. It was a less visible, less stressful position. I needed to setup various systems to perform the admin functions, and it wasn't moving fast as people who were supposed to help me setup my system were dragging their feet . . . .

Those who saw me in the downtown also seemed pretty excited about me . . . . One day, I wore a cute no-sleeve top, somewhat low cut, lower cut than what I usually wear, because it was very hot. I was standing in front of my tall building, smoking cigarette, and the guys walking by said, "She is totally out to shoot the foot now!" It seemed like everyone needed more excitement, I myself needed more excitement!

In a way, I thought I'd rather be treated equally for my intelligence and education, but most people seemed to prefer to give credit for my look. One of my old teammates, an old guy, said to his buddy on the phone, "You really have to see her to appreciate her! She's just got the right look!" However, what made me interesting to most people was my personality, I believed, since most people didn't get to see me (and just got interested in me reading my e-mails). Many referred me as a "Poet" or "Red Lips" or something along that line.

BMI people said that I would be a superb BMI'er. BMI had a lot of single guys, and most of the noticeable ones were German-Americans. The Engineering field has many German-Americans, in general, and BMI seemed to be full of them (more than any other organizations I had seen). Brad was a German-American, and Kevin was a German-American as well.

Kevin moved to the same building as one of my cubicle mates, and he became interested in the back going, interested in me . . . Unfortunately, he wasn't coming in to use the shared cube. Even if he did, it would never be the same day when I came in, so Kevin just worked from home. He was still doing the site design work, and I had no reason to interact with him. He was on the *sametime,* trying to send me signals, but it didn't feel right to contact him, not seeing him and not working with him.

Not long after I had moved to CNAGI Philadelphia facility, a GNI contacted me to inform me that BMI cutoff the funding for my task. I supported the BMI as a temp for less than 10 months . . .

Subject: Chaos with nobody following the rule

It's raining today, and I am feeling rainy myself, wondering if knowledge is power or pain? There are so many things that I wish I don' t know, but I keep learning and keep seeing more bad tactics (instead of good ones).

I chose to become an engineer to make a clean living (and to avoid the *people games* as much as possible), but somehow I got dragged into the dirtiest politics of all. For what I have seen, Americans are becoming too smart and too arrogant, full of bullshit. It's no longer "Ask not what others can do for you, ask what you can do for others",,, but it's more like ***take what you want with bullshit at someone else' expense!*** *Or hassle others (the cheapest kind) if your tummy hurts; I am not happy, so nobody can be happy mentality.*

I don't know what to think any more, I don't want to think. What good is thinking when the merits get twisted as the faults???? Some don't even try to twist, acting like it's their rights to go againt one's merit (using others' jealousy as the weapon), especially if one is a minority; She is smart, that's bad.. I don't get appreciated for coming up with a solution, I get hated for coming up with the solutions that they couldn't and get screwed as 15-, like it's the *right* thing.

Something is not working right here, not just for me (an Asian elite), but it seems like America is losing the good spirit with too big of individual ego's. Who carried the American Flag at the Beijing Olympic? Some guy who they borrowed from Kenya or wherever -- Something didn't look right there.

Time is crawling for me here now, watching the endless and meaningless ego-fight,,,,, and the bad part is that I am not sure how I could have done better or how to change it for better?

I wish I wasn't so smart. It's terrible to be smart to detect all these stupid or cheap tactics that people are playing . . . . I was pretty satisfied when I was naive, when I didn't know better. Maybe it's just one of the facts of life, becoming a cranky old woman, with all this 'not knowing is the medicine' knowledge.

In the IT industry, there are a lot of well-educated Asian engineers, so nobody made an ISSUE out of me being an Asian, but through television, it's a different matter. These people haven't seen too many engineers, and in fact, I may be the first engineer who they get to see? Other engineers would consider me as a rotten egg caught by the television, for good reasons (it's a PAIN to have someone watching you over with a magnifying glass).

America is going crazy, or maybe changing . . . . Changes always bring confusions and some extreme behaviors, I guess, and I happen to be one of those new kinds that they haven't seen, almost like someone from the Mars?

I get to see a whole bunch of ego-twisted people on television talking about me!!!!!!!!!!!!!!!!!!!!. Television is totally image-oriented, skin-deep, and the idiots who watch TV shows with very little knowledge learn things from the *TV jokes (about me)*,,, which is okay except it affects me in negative way.

One comedy show was making a big joke out of my case last Saturday, with a pregnant woman theme . . . Mom doesn't have a baby who wants to kill her, right? Mom may kill the baby she had, but I happen to be a good one, so that won't happen. Besides, they are blocking me from getting a job, so nothing is going to happen.

People make an ISSUE out of every e-mail I send (or don't send, stealing my e-mail scrabbles), and *some ridiculous people even try to corner me with security issue, for sending e-mails to my own sister, making something out of every little thing I say! That's beyond being PAIN!!* I also have seen some people who try to corner me as a crazy person, a *headcase*, so nothing surprises me anymore.

I am thankful to America for giving me many chances in my earlier years, having been generous, I would say. But lately, I don't know what to think, dunno why I am here??? All I get to see is *bullshit or hassle, making things extremely hard for me, impossible to get a job.*

Besides, doing a good job is not a merit for me anymore. So, what's the motivation? If I do a better job than the Whites (or the Blacks), I get kicked out as 15 (or get ignored). Some people, especially moms and the Blacks, are sooooooo abusing this *15 thing*, so abusing the *ganging-up's*, I am just dumb-found. Some of them are like "*You are better than me, I am going to harass you with 15-*" ganging-up with my kind" (215 is the law). Nobody follows the law and it results in a chaos, of course.

It should just be a matter of demand and supply naturally, but with all kinds of mumbo-jumbo's, racial conflicts, playing dirty number games, I am not sure if Einstein would have been able to find a solution for this mess . . .

There is an American saying, 'when going gets tough, tough gets going', and that was before the TV people learned about me. With television watching, it's more like *tough gets killed* . . .

It seems that everyone is trying to have some fun (with me/using me), and I am having trouble motivating myself in this negative territory. *I am wondering if it is the* territory that one cannot win.

Some people say that I am incredible referring me as 007, but being incredibly good only costs me my job. And it's taking me to nowhere (to poverty, actually), just getting kicked around. If one gets killed for being good at something, fxxx that thing!?

HARMONY AND HAPPINESS . . . . ?

During a self-confidence training that I received at BNS, the trainer asked everyone, "What makes us happy?" Someone answered, "love?" The trainer asked again, "Love is good, but what really makes us happy?" I answered, "Feeling good about yourself." And he said smiling at me, "YES! That's it! Feeling good about yourself, that's what this is all about." Everyone was looking at me, somewhat surprised and impressed, and one female, a Managing Consultant, said, "Oh, yea, it must be feeling good working hard with her tongue!" The trainer looked at me compassionately, and I just shrugged.

Regardless of this senior female's nasty putdown comment (with no ground what-so-ever), I felt GOOD about myself. When I feel good about myself, what others say or do in an attempt to put me down had very little affect on me. It's not pleasant, but it doesn't make me feel less. It was her who felt inferior and that was why she had to make such an irrelevant and ridiculous comment as an attempt to bring herself up by bringing me down, to make herself feel better.

I worked relatively closely with the HR Head both at Karlmon Dietech and ACIS. Both of them in their 50's with long HR experience, but their attitudes towards me were almost opposite. The Karlmon Dietech HR Director was interested in helping me dealing with being a female engineer in the male-dominated field whereas the ACIS HR just wanted to get rid of me even though I wasn't the one who initiated any of the back shooting activities, for being pressured and attacked by others. She treated me as the source of the trouble regardless of my willingness to cooperate with her. When one's intention is negative, nothing gets resolved if the situation doesn't get deteriorated, and in that case, the only option is to stay away from those with negative intention, unfortunately.

The Karlmon Dietech HR Head had called "happy man" rule to bring me back in, but their married executive secretary won people going against him with "family preference" (while she was playing the back herself). I would call it as being hypocritical.

For what I have experienced, most men would like to have someone special at work, someone who he could feel comfortable as a person. And the same goes for most women, I believe. The question is how can one control oneself and be able to keep a desirable working relationship (without emotions interfering with work or other personal matters/family)? And how can one selected as 316 avoid being victimized by the gang . . . ? Have fun and drop dead is not an option. I heard people commenting me as being remarkable getting 2 out of 3, but so far I learned that there is no 2 out of 3!!!!!!!!!!!!!!!!!!!!!!!!!!!!!!

Bosses, television people, or just regular guys (married or single), they all seemed to need more excitement, lacking something in their lives (or bored of their marriages), need someone to play with (26, 36) . . .

Too many people are insisting on *my kind only,* even *me only, otherwise I am going to be the hassle,* playing the "hassle-out" game. No compromise, no harmony. I've had the Black guys who supported me in the real working world, often nicer to me than the White guys, but those on television seem to try to generate the *Black-only* ganging-up immediately as if that's the right thing to do.

What I have seen in America through the television is the overbearing arrogance, "above the law" with air-blown ego, even trying to play the God (exercising their air power trying to mobilize their viewers to kill me, playing with the irresponsible-vague gestures and images). I would like to think that I was lucky enough to witness so full of cheap and dirty tactics people play against me! One does not become the winner with cheap tactics. One becomes the winner by learning from or embracing the other winner.

Married life is the best proven lifestyle but it is often boring, and that's why I got divorced one of the nicest guys in the world. I needed to search other option to be more content with my life. I felt like I had no life when I was married and needed more excitement.

Professional life can provide a break for the boring marriage, with an interesting working partner who can fill the missing or lacking part of the marriage life . . . For both men and women . . As for what I have seen, men are more willing to compromise for the harmony than women, in general.

Compromise is what is needed for harmony and happiness. Everyone needs to allow others to be happier, instead of trying to prevent someone from being happier than themselves. It would be better for the miserable ones to adapt the happier people's way than to try to bring down others to their misery level.

The idea of back is achieving a happier life while providing a better option for woman professionals in the male-dominated field, not for doing the fruitless, if not destructive, ego-competition.

Deviled Egg Report

www.ingramcontent.com/pod-product-compliance
Lightning Source LLC
Chambersburg PA
CBHW051225050326
40689CB00007B/809